AMERICA

☆ ☆

OVER THE WATER

Shirley Collins

"Shirley was, of course, the perfect person to take into the field because she loved every minute of it. She took wonderful notes, and was a huge help, was great with all the people and a perfect field companion. She helped me in hundreds of ways I didn't even know being an unobservant, busy male."

Alan Lomax, from an interview with Ken Hunt.

"I found it very touching indeed. You know from the writing that this is a woman of knowledge and sophistication... and you're suddenly aware that this person who you have been reading these very touching letters of, knows in her maturity all sorts of things about music and people and moralities. And it's very moving."

Sir David Attenborough

"Reading her book, I start to understand her better, and while she is typically self-effacing, she has been prompted to give away much more of herself than she might have chosen. Which of course makes it so much more interesting."

Maddy Prior (Steeleye Span), The Times

"Shirley Collins paints a vivid picture of two lost and contrasting worlds. Most unforgettable of all is her description of discovering the previously unknown Mississippi Fred McDowell. An absolute gem."

★ ★ ★ ★ Uncut

"She is a wonderfully laconic and informative raconteur. Masterpieces are seldom so readable. Contender for book of the year."

★ ★ ★ ★ Record Collector

"Collins is one of English traditional music's most celebrated voices and a fine writer too. In this frank, lively account she comes across as single-minded and tough, but also naive and unworldly. This only adds to the narrative's charm. A fascinating musicological documentary and a love story too. Best of all, a spine-tingling account of the first-ever recordings of Mississippi Fred McDowell."

★ ★ ★ ★ MOJO Magazine

"Her dramatic snapshot memories drip with atmosphere. A thoroughly enjoyable memoir and a valuable addition to our understanding of the music." *The Wire Magazine*

"A gem of a book." (50 Best Books of the Year)

Bookmarks, London

AMERICA

★ ★

OVER THE WATER

Shirley Collins

saf publishing

saf publishing

First published in hardback 2005 by SAF Publishing
Paperback edition: 2007. First edition.

SAF Publishing Ltd.
149 Wakeman Road,
London. NW10 5BH
ENGLAND

email: info@safpublishing.com
www.safpublishing.com

ISBN 10: 0 946719 91 8
ISBN 13: 978 0 946719 91 4

Author photograph: Katie Vandyck

A CIP catalogue record for this book is available from the British Library

Cover design: David Nobakht

Printed in England by the Cromwell Press, Trowbridge, Wiltshire

For my mother, Dorothy Florence Collins, for Polly Marshall, Robert Marshall, Joe Miller-Marshall, Louis Miller-Marshall, Amanita Dolly Collins, Lisa Miller, Sam Collins, Chris Taplin and as ever, Pip Barnes, my dearest friend for the last 28 years.

With love to Tina and Vic Smith, and Rebe and Dan Quinn.

Remembering Dolly Collins and Buz Collins.

In memory of Alan Lomax (1915-2002), arguably the world's leading folklorist, who collected in the USA, the British Isles, Spain, Italy and the Caribbean.

Acknowledgements

With love and thanks to Malcolm Taylor OBE, Ian Kearey, David Suff, David Tibet and David Keenan.

And to my publishers Dave Hallbery and Mick Fish.

Thanks to Anna Lomax Wood and The Association for Cultural Equity and the Alan Lomax Archive in New York for willingly and generously allowing us to have photographs and the recording logs.

The publishers would also like to thank Bertram Lyons of The Alan Lomax Archive for his valuable assistance in photographic research.

www.culturalequity.org

Photographic Credits

All photographs from the Spanish trip in 1953 and the Southern Journey trip of 1959 were taken by Alan Lomax, with the exception of those with Alan in the photo, which were taken by Shirley Collins. These photographs and the Recording Logs which start on page 196 are courtesy of The Association of Cultural Equity and the Alan Lomax Archive.

All photographs of Shirley Collins' family and early years are from her own collection.

Contents

Foreword

by David Tibet

I DO NOT KNOW HOW TO INTRODUCE A BOOK AS IMPORTANT AS this is to me except to state that, of those artists whose music I have loved and whose work I have followed with so much joy and excitement over many years, Shirley and her work holds a particularly prominent place in my heart.

I remember the moment I first heard her sing, whilst I was in a flat in Clapham, with the sound of traffic and the sight of decay in the streets around me. A friend had told me to buy *Love, Death and the Lady* by Shirley and Dolly Collins. At hearing that first line in the title track, sung in a voice innocent and despairing, profound and simple, I realised I had come across someone whose art would change my life: "*As I walked out one morn in May, the birds did sing and the lambs did play, I met an old man by the way*".

I obtained every album and single by Shirley and her sister that I could find; I realised how little I knew about her life and her work outside of the recordings themselves. There was evidently a rapid and determined progression from the sparse and unadorned singing and arrangements of the first early singles (on the Collector label) and her first albums, (on the American Folkways and English Decca labels) *False True Lovers* and *Sweet England*, to the splendour of *The Power of the True Love Knot*, *Anthems in Eden* and *Love, Death and the Lady*, in which mediaeval, baroque, psychedelic, and folk music all rushed together to form a structure of heart-breaking beauty. I also found her name on a large number of albums, anthologies of field recordings of American and British music, compiled with Alan Lomax, of whom I then knew nothing.

Eventually I met Shirley and Dolly, discovering to my surprise and sadness that they had retired as a duo, and that Shirley, then living in Brighton, had given up any idea of ever recording again, although Dolly was still composing music, notably her *Humanist Mass* with words by the poet Maureen Duffy, *The Pity Of War*, a suite of settings of first world War poems, and a new arrangement of *The Beggar's Opera* which she had completed just before her unexpected death in Sussex in 1995. Over many conversations with Shirley—for she was unbecomingly self-effacing about her achievement, and seemingly unaware of how important her work was to so many people (not to mention the exorbitant prices that her records commanded)—I found out more about her fascinating story. Her journey, into the very essence itself of English song, occurred during an amazing life.

Born in pre-World War Two Hastings to a family of singers, scholars, activists and characters, she went on journeys to Warsaw and Moscow, travelled to the Appalachians, recorded prisoners at the notorious Parchman Farm, was present at the discovery of the wondrous Mississippi Fred McDowell, and all of this before returning to England, still very young, to create, with her sister Dolly, one of the most powerful and emotional bodies of work of which I know, and collaborating with luminaries such as David Munrow, The Incredible String Band, Peter Bellamy, and many other pivotal figures. Shirley told me, many years after we first met, that she was writing the memoirs of her time spent travelling and collecting songs in the States with Alan Lomax. I was delighted to receive the first draft, but on reading it, felt it was only half-accurate, missing out so much of what I wanted to read about her own life and experience in North America. She had left out practically all information on herself, and the book read as an account of Alan Lomax's quest, with a retiring young girl from Sussex assisting, who occasionally mentioned herself. It seemed to me to be a great injustice to a woman whose influence and art has so greatly affected so many people, both musicians and listeners, within the folk world and without. Over many re-writings, Shirley thankfully overcame her modesty to write this luminous account of her time in America, interspersed with memories of her family life and how she entered the world of folk music.

This book is a touching and important document; an account of the meeting of different cultures in different times seen through the eyes of a charismatic and courageous woman who, researching these often ignored expressions of the outcast and marginal, asserted the profound humanity of those who gave voice to it. In these pages we see that the spirit of the deepest and simplest beauty abides in small places.

It is also about a woman whose quiet determination and unending interest in people and their stories add tremendously to what we know about the 1959 field trip. Shirley also changed absolutely the world of English folk song by what she brought into it; and her influence increases.

She is our nearest star. Thank you.

David Tibet / Current 93,
London, March 17, 2004.

ALAN LOMAX

"Ascoltate, le colline cantano!"

*Shirley,
I wish I'd found you
singing on one of these
singing hills.
Alan*

Estratto dalla Rivista dell' Accademia Nazio-
nale di Santa Cecilia - Anno V N. 4 1956
R O M A

Hark, the Hills are Singing, Alan Lomax's booklet on folksong collecting
in Italy, with the inscription: *"Shirley, I wish I'd found you singing on one of
these singing hills. Alan."*

1

The Beginning

THEY HAD LAIN IN A DRAWER AT MY MOTHER'S HOUSE FOR many years, my letters from America. I'd posted them home back in 1959, the year I lived in the States with the American folklorist Alan Lomax. In the late summer we made an historic field trip, making record-ings of folk music in the deep country of the rural South, several of which, some forty years later would end up being sampled by contemporary American musician Moby, showing up in the Coen Brothers' film, *O Brother Where Art Thou*, in Martin Scorsese's *Gangs of New York* and on Ry Cooder's CD of the soundtrack of *The Long Riders*.

It was a journey that started in Virginia, and took us into Parchman Farm, the notorious Mississippi State Penitentiary, up Kentucky mountainsides to record Primitive Baptist open-air prayer meetings, to the heart of Alabama for the Sacred Harp Convention, into tiny hamlets in the tornado belt of rural Arkansas where the pioneering spirit still existed, and into isolated black communities in Northern Mississippi where we discovered one of the finest hitherto unknown bluesmen, ending our journey on one of the Georgia Sea Islands that had been settled by escaped slaves.

People, and certainly those of my working class background, didn't travel much in the 1950s, and to go to America was virtually unheard of. My letters home form the basis of this book, and reflect how things were then. They may well seem naïve nowadays, when we can all jet off at the drop of a credit card to world-wide holiday destinations.

"So where do you come from, young lady?"

"I'm from England."

"What—England over the water?"

Elderly mountaineer in Kentucky

So how *did* a girl from Sussex fetch up in America with America's leading folklorist?

2

Leaving Home—London 1953

IN THE LATE AUTUMN OF 1953, KNOWING THAT ABOVE ALL I wanted to be a folk singer, I decided to move to London where I could sing and research songs in the Cecil Sharp Library, now known as the Ralph Vaughan Williams Library, at Cecil Sharp House, the home of The English Folk Dance and Song Society. The library wasn't the friendly and welcoming place it is nowadays under the librarian Malcolm Taylor OBE (recently honoured and deservedly so), and you had to take your courage in your hands to brave your way in. The disapproval was almost palpable.

I found a job at a bookshop in Belsize Park, rented a bedsitter, lived on a diet of buns and tinned soup, became undernourished, getting painful chilblains on my heels that first winter. I spent what was left of my meagre wages (29 shillings and 6 pence a week—the equivalent of £1.50p) on books of folksongs, and all my spare time at Cecil Sharp House. Thank goodness, Peter Kennedy, son of the Director of the English Folk Dance and Song Society, and a collector for the BBC, was trying to make the House more welcoming and accessible to young people, and he and John Hasted, a physics professor at University College, encouraged us by giving us an informal space where we could sing. More importantly, they brought up to London old traditional singers for us to listen to and learn from. The great ones were still alive—Harry Cox from Norfolk, Bob Roberts from Suffolk, and George Maynard from Sussex, whom I especially loved. He reminded me so much of Granddad, who had died while I was away at college. He sang wonderful songs such as "Polly On the Shore" and "Our Captain Calls All Hands", songs which struck me to the heart. I still think him the greatest English singer. I heard Seamus Ennis, the magical Irish uileann pipe player, and the remarkable travellers Margaret Barry, Phoebe Smith and Davy Stewart. I soaked up the singing and the styles.

The folk scene was gradually opening up in London, and the most famous of the clubs was The Troubadour in Earl's Court, a coffee bar owned by two charismatic Canadians, Mike and Sheila Van Bloemen. At one point they gave me a job waitressing in the coffee bar, where Richard Harris was a daily customer, making a coffee and a newspaper last all morning. Singers came from far and wide to sing there. Alex Campbell was always welcome, as was the young Martin Carthy. Our favourite Americans were Derroll Adams and Rambling Jack Elliott, complete with cowboy hats and boots and a laconic western style of singing, a bit reminiscent of Woody Guthrie. So when a young interloper turned up and sang pretty much like them both, I didn't reckon much of him,

I was the runner-up in a folk singing competition at Cecil Sharp House circa 1955.

and didn't think much of his chances as a singer. His name was Bob Dylan. I'd better confess at this point that I also had the same opinion about Paul Simon, who appeared bottom of the bill at the De La Warr Pavilion in Bexhill (if my memory serves me right). Appearing above him were "THE WATERSON QUARTET ON THEIR NATION-WIDE TOUR (I think they'd just come down from Hull!) and SHIRLEY COLLINS—ENGLAND'S VERSATILE YOUNG INSTRUMENTALIST (I could play six chords on the banjo). And yes, I did revise my opinion about both of them.

Alan Lomax in Spain, 1953.

My circle of acquaintances gradually widened. I met Ewan McColl, a leading figure of the Folk Revival, and was invited to go to Warsaw to sing at a World Youth Peace Festival. I was familiar with the sights of bomb damage at home, but I was shocked by how the walls of buildings in Warsaw were pock-marked with hundreds of bullet holes, and by how utterly desolate and unnervingly silent was the concentration camp we were taken to visit.

A couple of years later I was off to Moscow. It was a memorable journey—and when we changed trains at the Polish border and climbed up into the big Russian train

I was thrilled to see a huge red star on the front of the engine. At that time, Stalin was still Uncle Joe to me, the name we'd known him by throughout the war. On our journey across Russia the train stopped occasionally at little halts, where groups of people offered us flowers and badges and beakers of hot black tea sweetened with a spoonful of jam. I was very touched by these encounters—it didn't occur to me then that they might have been orchestrated—and quickly learned to say "hello" and "thank you" and "peace and friendship" in Russian. Our wooden slatted seats were hard, but the thrill of the journey outweighed the discomfort. What *was* difficult was chewing my way through leather-tough garlic sausage, my first experience of such food, and trying to eat a bowl of clear soup with a whole hard-boiled egg rolling about in it, using only a spoon, as the train lurched along.

I was in Moscow to sing and I was taking part in a concert in the Kremlin. I should have remarkable memories of this but all I can now recall is sitting waiting for my turn to sing and having a premonition that the girl I was sharing a hotel room with was stealing my money which I had foolishly left behind. Sure enough, when I got back it was gone. Luckily I had two nylon slips with me which I sold on the black market, and was solvent again. I was in a production of a ballad opera that Ewan had written for Joan Littlewood's Theatre Workshop, replacing the singer and actress Isla Cameron who was ill. But I was inexperienced, and my lack of interest in acting inevitably made the association short-lived.

On my return to London from Moscow, I accepted an invitation from Ewan MacColl to a party he was throwing for Alan Lomax, who was coming back to England after two years collecting folk songs in Spain and Italy. I already knew of Alan through his series of folk music radio programmes for the BBC—*Adventures of a Ballad Hunter* produced by a young David Attenborough. He played field recordings made by him and his father John in America for the Library of Congress. I remembered how enthralled I was by both the music and Alan's accent.

So the invitation threw me into a panic at the prospect of meeting my hero. What would I wear? I had so few clothes, so little money. I decided to make myself a skirt. This was rather optimistic of me, since I'd never even been able to finish a shoe-bag or a pillow-slip in sewing lessons at school. The material I chose for my skirt was navy needlecord, a reasonably fine one, but I must have looked a bit of a bundle in it.

However, at the party, there Alan Lomax was, an affable, tall, solid Texan with a big head of shaggy dark hair, and he put me in mind of an American bison. I blurted out that one of my ambitions was to go to the Library of Congress to hear his field recordings, and he said he was amazed that I even knew about it. He had great warmth and an irresistible chuckle. I fell in love, and he seemed to like me too, in spite of my skirt.

Reader I didn't marry him, but after a short courtship, I went to live with him in Highgate. During this time, Alan was completing his *Columbia World Folk Music* series and his book for Cassell, *The Folk Songs of North America*. I was his editorial assistant, and his lover, although I was very nervous of the fact. Things were different then. I was embarrassed and afraid of what people would think. I'd much rather have been married, as living together was unheard of at least in the circles I'd been used to moving in.

My copy of Alan's American Anthropologist publication *Folk Song Style* inscribed:

Dear Special Asst –
You must have typed this 9 times at least. And lived through it a score of times. Thanks for your patience in truth. C.Seeger has written that he has been able to find only one flaw in it. A mis-called mountain range. My Gawd!
Love Alan.

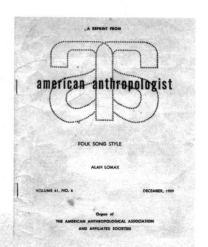

A REPRINT FROM

american anthropologist

FOLK SONG STYLE

ALAN LOMAX

VOLUME 61, NO. 6   DECEMBER, 1959

Organ of
THE AMERICAN ANTHROPOLOGICAL ASSOCIATION
AND AFFILIATED SOCIETIES

Dear Special Asst —
You must have typed this
9 times at least. And lived
through it a score y times. Thanks
for your patience in truth.
C. Seeger has written that he
has been able to find only one
flaw in it. A mis-called mt.
range. My Gawd!

Love

Alan

They were busy and eventful times, the house often full of visiting American bluesmen—Sonny Terry and Brownie McGhee, Memphis Slim and Muddy Waters, for whom Alan cooked a special Southern dinner of fried chicken and smothered greens to make him feel at home. It tasted wonderful, but looking back I wonder if it wasn't a little patronising of Alan. Still, it could have been worse—he could have cooked chitterlings and corn pone.

Another friend of Alan's, an American living in Hampstead, was the screenwriter Donald Ogden Stewart. It was many years later I learned that he wrote the screenplay for one of my favourite films, *The Philadelphia Story*.

Life wasn't without its difficulties though. We were sharing the flat with his ten-year old daughter Anne, his ex-wife Elizabeth and her partner Herb, who were writing a book about Spain, and inevitably there were problems. I don't think I coped too well. I was too young and unworldly. Alan was twenty years older than me, and I was only ten years older than his daughter. It must have been hard for Anne to have both her parents under the same roof, but living with other partners. I was nervous of Elizabeth, I felt she resented me being there, and she was a fiery, proud Texan. I was hopelessly inexperienced in things domestic. Elizabeth was a wonderful cook; her Texan and Spanish dishes were a revelation to me.

The good food revolution was still many years away. All I knew how to cook was liver and onions, which they all refused to eat, to my great bewilderment, as they believed it would give them liver flukes, and a dish called "sukey" which Granny used to make. You put milk in a saucepan,

Opposite: At the flat in Highgate.

added chopped up cheddar cheese, a knob of butter and white pepper (the only sort there was available then), put it on the heat and stirred it till the cheese was melted and stringy, and then you poured it over toast. It did make the toast soggy, but we'd loved it as children. I remember the first time I produced it for the Lomaxes there was a silence at the table, Elizabeth's lips pursed in scorn as she prodded the mass with her fork, and even the quaint old English name of "sukey" couldn't redeem it. I did pick up one of her recipes which I still love today, *huevos rancheros*—fried eggs topped with chopped fresh tomato, garlic and chilli.

My twenty-first birthday was coming up, and I hoped that Alan would give me a gold watch—wasn't that what everyone received when they reached twenty-one? We'd arranged a party, and I spent the day preparing. In the middle of the afternoon Alan said he had to go out. I was so excited, wondering what he was planning. The party and the guests came and went, but Alan didn't show up. He came back in the early hours of the morning, and told me he had spent the evening with an old flame, Robin Roberts, a beautiful American folk singer who was visiting London. I don't remember what, if anything, he gave me, but it certainly wasn't a watch, gold or otherwise. I was hurt and I was angry, and I went home to Hastings. There was no telephone there, of course, so I was completely out of touch.

A few days had passed when a knock came at the door. It was a contrite Alan, asking me to go back to him. He made it up to me by taking me for a holiday in France, visiting the chateaux of the Loire, first stopping off in Paris for a couple of days to visit Gilbert Rouget, director of the Musée de l'Homme,

FORM OF CONTRACT BETWEEN ALAN LOMAX AND PETER KENNEDY

We, the undersigned do hereby agree to act under partnership in relation to folk music recordings made by us in Britain during the last eight years for the purpose of selling such material to Record Companies.

Signed ....(Alan Lomax)

28.6.58
London,.England......   ....*Peter Kennedy*......(Peter Kennedy)

Miss Shirley Collins is hereby commissioned to act as my personal representative in relation to editing these tapes into records during my absence from Great Britain, and it is my understanding that my share of the advances be paid to her as salary up to the extent of one hundred pounds for her services in connexion with editing these tapes.

The tapes referred to are 226 seven inch reels of recordings made by me in various parts of the British Isles and are being left by me in charge of Miss Shirley Collins, who is to work with Peter Kennedy on this project. Other parties may not have access to these tapes without my written permission.

Alan Lomax

Alan Lomax's contract with Peter Kennedy and me, 1958.

Back in London we continued to live together, working on the Columbia World Folk Song Series of LPs and the book *The Folk Songs of North America* for Cassell, in which Alan credited me as Editorial Assistant. Alan and Peter Kennedy recorded in two days the thirty-seven songs that would make up my first two solo LPs, *Sweet England* for Decca in London, and *False True Lovers* for Folkways in the States. When the

June 28th, 1958.

To whom it may concern:

This is a letter of recommendation for Miss Shirley Collins, who has been acting as my secretary and editorial assistant for the past two and a half years. She has been directly concerned in the following projects, doing typing, secretarial work, research, proof-reading and editorial work.

1) Penguin Book of American Folk Songs, to be published in Spring, 1959.
2) The Folk Songs of North America, Cassell, 1959. A book of three hundred songs and one hundred throusand words.
3) Two series of programs for the BBC: - Recollections of a Ballad Hunter, and A Ballad Hunter Looks at Britain.... Fourteen hours of broadcasting.
4)   LPs of schòlarly nature: Nixa, Blues in the Mississippi Night; Nixa: Murderer's Home; Nixa: American Song Train; EMI: Great American Ballads; Melodisc: Texas Folk-Songs; Tradition: Folk Songs of Italy; Tradition: Folk Songs of Scotland; Tradition: Negro Prison Songs; Westminster: Eleven LPs covering the folk music of Spain.

This in addition to a great volume of research correspondence with people scattered around the world, and work in catalogueing and transcribing the material from a large collection of British tape recordings.

Miss Collins is not only a flexible, cheerful and hard-working person, but she has a special flair for literary work . She is a very fast reader and an excellent proof-reader. She can also take the initiative of correcting and polishing copy as she works. Most of all, she has a great interest and infectious enthusiasm for anything connected with writing and with books. Anyone who has her help in the capacity of editorial assistant will be lucky indeed.

The standard of coffee-making is high I

Alan Lomax.

Alan's letter of recommendation for me, written prior to his return to the US.

work was done, Alan decided to return to the States alone. I waved him a heartbroken goodbye one July day in 1958 at Waterloo Station. To try to comfort me, Mum bought a box of chocolates and took me to a cinema in Leicester Square to see *Attila the Hun*, starring Sophia Loren. That night she put me to bed with a cup of tea and an aspirin. It was the days of simple remedies.

Alan and I kept in touch over the next few months, and one day a letter arrived from him saying that he would like me to join him in the States. He was planning a collecting trip in the South and wanted me as his assistant. This was a dream come true, an ambition that I had never thought would be fulfilled. My favourite songbook had long been Cecil Sharp's *English Folk Songs from the Southern Appalachians*, (63 shillings I paid for the two volumes, more than two weeks' wages at Collett's Bookshop).

The books were the result of three field trips he undertook there with Maud Karpeles from 1916-18. They collected over sixteen hundred different tunes in Kentucky, North Carolina, Virginia and Tennessee, some of the most exquisite songs and some of the finest versions of British ballads ever found. To me, the survival of those songs, over hundreds of years and across thousands of miles, was and still is a miracle, and now I was to have the opportunity to experience it at first hand. Where Sharp and Karpeles had used notebooks and manuscript paper, we would be using tape recorders, and I would be visiting the South at last.

I boarded the SS United States in April 1959 and went over the water to America.

3

The Voyage Out

Well met, well met, you old true love
Well met, well met, said she
I've just come in from the salt, salt sea
From the land where the grass grows green

THE 5-DAY VOYAGE WAS WONDERFUL. THE LINER WAS LUXURI-
ous, and the food unbelievable. "Austerity" was still the
word in England, but not here. Fresh exotic fruit for breakfast, fruit that I had never seen outside a tin, eggs cooked
in ways I'd never heard of. I tried "shirred" eggs to find to
my disappointment that they were scrambled eggs pushed
into a ridged pattern—or perhaps my unsophisticated palate
couldn't register the subtlety that defined "shirred". It occurs
to me now, that there may have been a misprint on the menu,
and the word should have been 'stirred'—perhaps that is
what Americans call scrambled eggs. There were thick beef

steaks, turkey—the first I had ever eaten (even chicken had up to very recently been a treat that we had only at Christmas at home), and there was seafood. In Hastings I'd only ever eaten fish and the tiny shrimps and cockles that came fresh from the Channel and which we ate doused in vinegar. I tried lobster, clams, fat American shrimp, delicious dressings and sauces, and loved it all. England was still in the culinary Dark Ages in 1959, at least for someone of my background and purse. Alan had taken me to Spanish and Italian restaurants in London, so I wasn't quite a novice, but even so, the varieties of food and the huge portions available on board were amazing to me. Just as well there were deck games and a swimming pool so that you could burn off a little of the last feast before tackling the next. I loved being on the ocean and spent hours on deck just gazing across the water.

I was happy and excited, but I was also scared. This was the 1950s after all, a time of extreme anti-Communism in America, with the Un-American Activities Committee supremely powerful. Alan, himself a left-winger, had fled the States to escape the witch-hunt, and had been in trouble with the fascist authorities in Spain. My mother was involved with the Communist Party in Hastings, and I had been to Poland and to Russia with the World Youth Peace Festival. In order to get an entry visa for the States, I had lied on my application form, and denied any connection with prohibited left-wing organisations. Because of Alan's associations and his status as a single man, he wasn't able to sponsor me, so his agent and his agent's wife had agreed to act as my sponsors, although we had never met. All this preyed on my mind. I was so afraid I was going to be questioned by Immigration and refused entry, or sent to Ellis Island.

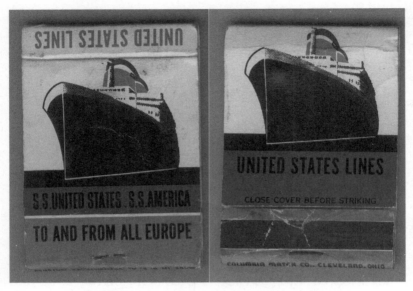

My souvenir matchbooks from the SS United States.

We came in to New York as dawn was breaking. The sight of the Statue of Liberty in the pale light was profoundly stirring, and as we passed her I sent up to her impassive gaze a prayer to help me through. I thought of all the poor hopeful and fearful immigrants in the past who must have done the same, people at the end of journeys full of danger and hardship, and with far more at stake. The ship was a long time docking, but finally we disembarked. Alan was there, smiling and waving, with his daughter Anne. How infinitely dear they looked to me. All I had to do was get through Immigration. The queue was long and slow-moving, and the officers were stern and unsmiling. Could they hear my heart pounding? Still, I managed to answer their questions calmly enough. They accepted my papers and let me through. I hurled myself into Alan's arms. My American adventure had begun.

We drove to 121 West 3rd Street in an old green Ford. Its right-hand front door flew open when we went round sharp curves, but if you held on tight to the handle, the door stayed closed most of the time. I was a bit disappointed with Alan's flat, which wasn't quite as smart as I'd imagined it would be. It was on the top floor of a narrow five-storey building above a Pizza Parlour. There was just one large room, with tapes and books everywhere, one bedroom, a tiny kitchen and steps up to the flat roof where you could sunbathe.

The early days were a blur of meeting people, coming to terms with the cockroaches in the kitchen (just a black flash at the skirting boards when you switched the lights on), learning how to make coffee to Alan's taste—no Camp Coffee here—and becoming used to the heat of the New York spring. I had my first taste of pizza from the parlour below. I'd never seen a pizza cook whirl the dough on his fingertips to thin it and shape it (rather in the way a Chinese juggler spins plates on the end of a stick) and slide the pizzas in and out of the oven with a huge wooden paddle, and slip them into those big flat boxes. It seemed so exotic, and such fun.

The Italian owners were friendly and voluble, and they'd give me tastes of the various types of sausage and olives they used, and occasionally tease me with a really hot titbit. They adored Alan because he knew Italy, could speak some Italian, and besides, we were good customers. I had my first avocado, known in the States as an alligator pear. I'd never even seen one before. The taste and texture were strange and tantalising. I wasn't sure if I liked it, but I tried again and was hooked for life. Ice-cream was another revelation. I was amazed and overjoyed at the variety of flavours you could get. Howard Johnson made twenty-eight, all delicious and in such crunchy sweet thick cones. Back home you could only get synthetic vanilla, strawberry or chocolate. The only disappointment was American chocolate bars and cookies which I didn't like at all—just as well really.

The first time I went out alone I got lost, and made the embarrassing mistake of asking a traffic cop for directions. In New York, if you want to know the way or the time, you *don't* ask a policeman. I'd never been yelled at in public before, and I felt both foolish and scared. But that was the only hostile reaction I remember. Alan's friends were welcoming and hospitable. Looking back I wonder what they thought of our relationship. I was unworldly and twenty years his junior. What I had in my favour was youth, energy, intelligence, a capacity for hard work and an innately sound instinct and understanding of the music we both loved.

4

Hastings 1935—The Family

I WAS BORN IN 1935 IN THE SOUTH COAST TOWN OF HASTINGS into a close-knit working class family—a family that shaped me. My grandfather, Frederick Ball, had been Head Gardener on a large private estate in the hamlet of Telham, just outside Battle in East Sussex. He and Granny had five children, all of whom were carried outdoors in Granddad's arms as newborns to be shown the sky and trees and to hear the birdsong. Not that the babies would have been aware of course, but it meant a lot to Granddad who loved the countryside.

Granny saw the act as a bit of romantic flim-flam. She was less keen on country living, preferring life in town, away from the isolation and the mud, and it's understandable, as she coped for five years on her own when Granddad was sent as a soldier to India shortly after the birth of their fifth child in 1916. She took comfort in reading Dickens to her children in their tiny tied-cottage in the winter evenings, and they all survived the flu epidemic of 1918. Although the lady of the big house knew that the whole family was ill, the only help she gave was to order Cook to send down a blancmange. It was made entirely of water, with no milk or sugar, and left on the doorstep. This gesture probably hastened the family's recovery, as Gran's stubborn nature would have made her determined to survive such an insult.

Their children all grew up with a love of the countryside and of the arts, and a passion for cricket. The oldest son, Fred Ball, wrote about the family in his books *A Breath of Fresh Air* and *A Grotto for Miss Maynier*. He was also the biographer of Robert Tressell, author of *The Ragged Trousered Philanthropists*, the classic working-class novel of the early 1900s set in Mugsborough, a thinly disguised Hastings.

Robin Ball, R.A., a professional artist, became a war artist during World War II, while on active service in Belgium, and some of his drawings are housed at The Imperial War Museum. Grace, an amateur sculptor and painter, Fred and Robin are all dead, and only my mother, Dorothy Florence, an amateur writer, and her younger brother George, a painter living in Spain, survive.

The family formed the nucleus of the choir at the tiny church at Telham, christened Battle Cathedral by a local wit. Of them all, only Gran had some inclination towards religion, the rest being firm sceptics, but their attendance at church was compulsory. An almost feudal system still existed in rural England in the earlier part of the 20th century, and both the family's home and living were at stake.

> "I trust we shall see the children at Sunday School,
> and yourself at church," said the lady of the big house,

Grace, Dorothy and George outside Telham Hill Cottage, Nov 11, 1918.

and Granddad's employer. "Where did you normally worship?"

"Well," began mother, "Uh—we hadn't been goin' to church while the children were small..."
Mother didn't say that they went to music-hall while Granny minded the babies, it would have sounded irreverent.

"Oh you will like our little church," said the lady. "I have spoken to your husband about it."

(from *A Breath of Fresh Air,* FC Ball)

Still, however much they minded, they all loved to sing. One of the most comforting memories of my early childhood is of the family gatherings at Christmas, listening to the

A family portrait sent to Granddad while he was serving in India in 1917.
My mother is second from the left.

carols strengthened by the rich harmonies of the tenor and bass parts sung with great good humour and gusto by my uncles and granddad. At Aunt Grace's, too, on Boxing Day and New Year's Eve, we'd form up in two lines and dance "Sir Roger de Coverley" in her front room, all of us singing the tune except when it was our turn to gallop down the middle, Uncle George always pushing the tune on faster and faster.

A favourite song of Granny's at Christmas was "The Mistletoe Bough", the Gothic story of a young bride who, while playing hide-and-seek on her wedding day, hides in an old oak chest. The heavy lid closes fast, and the bride is never found, leaving Lord Lovell her husband to mourn her for many years. Tears trickled down our cheeks as Gran sang:

See the old man weeps for his fair young bride.
O the mistletoe bough, O the mistletoe bough.

Under his breath, Granddad, who although a compassionate man was not a sentimental one, chorused:

O that mis'rable row, O that mis'rable row!

"Fred! Stop that!" Gran hissed, digging her elbow in his ribs.

They sang a lot; Granddad liked old country songs, Granny favoured music-hall songs and often sang my sister Dolly and me to sleep when we were snug in her air-raid shelter during the War. She called it keeping our spirits up, but her good intentions were often undermined by her choice of songs from the Great War or sorrowful Edwardian ballads, made even more mournful by her rather quavery voice. Granddad played a tin whistle, but Granny was a bit grander with her harmonium, an instrument which fascinated Dolly and me, as the carpeted foot bellows which it was our job to pedal were labelled "Mouseproof". It was Gran who taught Dolly to play, thus launching her on her career as a composer and arranger, and I'm sure the churchy harmonies the family sang had a great influence on her.

5

The Train to California

Early July, 1959

Dear Mum and Dolly

So—I have travelled the Overland Trail of the western pioneers, I have crossed the Great Divide, flown in a jet, been bitten by a spider and a million mosquitoes so big you can't swat them with anything smaller than a tennis racquet.

But first... we left New York on June 20th, got in our beautiful new (to us) car—a second-hand 1951 Buick—cost 250 dollars, runs like a bird, or rather smoother than that—birds tend to hop, don't they! It's got a ventilation system that works—pull out the stops and the car is filled with cool air—you couldn't cope with the heat otherwise. We drove down through stinking chemical-factory and oil-plant ridden New Jersey and onto the Pennsylvania Turnpike which runs alongside the green, purple and blue tree-covered mountains of Pennsylvania for miles and miles, or cutting through them in long, long tunnels. Then onto the Turnpikes of Ohio, Iowa, Indiana, and finally the Illinois Turnpike into Chicago. We had left New York at eleven in the morning and driven eight hundred miles to Chicago, in eighteen hours, arriving there at 5 a.m. The turnpike ends at the bridge into the City which in turn merges into the main streets running for miles through the Negro section of town. And then there we were in the centre of Chicago which surprised me with its beauty. The orange sun was just rising and tinting the waters of Lake Michigan.

We were staying with Studs Terkel and his wife Ida who live very near the Lake. Studs is a radio man, short and greying, who gives off as much energy as the sun, crackling and sparkling like a firework, very restless, with bright, wise and friendly eyes. Ida put us straight to bed, and we slept till ten, then had breakfast outside on their wooden porch. It was a wonderful feast of link sausages, eggs, bacon, sliced tomatoes, peppers and spring onions (scallions they call them), blueberry muffins, cottage cheese, coffee and cream and a coffee cake stuffed with raisins and pecans, with a topping of caramelised cinnamon sugar. We almost fell through the floorboards we ate so much! (About link sausages: first time I heard them called that was when we stopped at a roadhouse to eat, and Alan ordered sausages. I heard the waitress ask him if he wanted Lynx. I was horrified!)

That afternoon, Alan and I recorded a programme with Studs about the projected recording trip South, then at 5 in the evening, leaving the precious Buick with the Terkels for safekeeping, we boarded a big yellow train, destination California and the Berkeley Folk Festival.

Alan, darling Alan had booked us a first-class compartment of our own, nobody to disturb us, two comfortable wide berths, chairs, our own toilet unit— luxury, luxury, luxury. And the food on the train! I mean, even the breakfasts were out of this world! To start, a choice of strawberries, raspberries, cantaloupe and honeydew melons, figs, prunes, blueberries......a choice from a dozen cereals, followed by eggs with ham, sausage, bacon, fish, with toast or muffins, french rolls or sweet rolls, pancakes, wheatcakes, and perfect coffee! All this on a train! For breakfast! But even so, by one o'clock you're ready for lunch, and off you go again, and it's even better! Turkey with cranberry sauce, mountain trout, T-bone steak. And nothing to do in between meals but sit in your own private room gazing first at each other and then at the scenery. Well, you both know what Alan looks like, so I'll tell you about the country.

The train speeds out of Chicago, and soon you are out on the Prairies, farming country—very flat, sparsely populated, all sky it seems. At least, you think it's flat at first, but when you get further West and deeper into the Prairies, it gets even flatter, something you wouldn't have thought was possible. The first evening, we sped through this land. Around nine o'clock, it was getting dark and very still. Then I became aware of the millions of fire-flies out there, wonderful little lights in the dark. Alan called them lightning bugs, and there was sheet lightning, too, that lit up the sky as far as you could see, every minute or so. We were still desperately tired after our long drive from New York, so we drew our curtains early and slept.

When we woke the next morning we were still in the Prairies, and we'd stopped at the old cow-town of Cheyenne. We had a twenty minute halt here, so we hopped out to have a quick look round. It was exciting to see men riding horses and wearing ten-gallon hats, and standing in the station yard, the last covered wagon to go west. And although the land still seemed flat, we had been climbing all the time while we'd been asleep. The altitude in Chicago is 614 feet, in Cheyenne it's 6060 feet, and ahead of us were the mountains—the front ranges of The Rockies and the Laramie Range. We had travelled from Illinois across the Mississippi River (I hadn't realised it ran so far North and West) into Iowa, Nebraska and Wyoming, past places named Squaw Creek, Bear River, Indian Creek, Skunk River, Coon Rapids and Mosquito Creek. Now the scenery began to get rugged with impressive buttes, and we were climbing quickly. By the time we got to Laramie, we had risen to 7151 feet above sea level—that's the highest point the train goes through.

All the rest of the day we crossed these ranges and The Great Divide, country so wild you wonder how the pioneers ever made it through. Gradually, it became desert. We passed through the tip of the Red Desert, across more mountains, through Bitter Creek, following all the time the path of the Overland Trail. Some of the rocks are such fantastic shapes and colours, it feels like being alive in a primeval age.... and the spaces are so overwhelmingly vast here. The train speeds for hours through this semi-desert mountain region and these mountains are not wooded or snowy, but rocky, of brown, red, green and white stone. There is very little water, even the so-called rivers here look like trickles in the wilderness. Occasionally you spot a lone settlement right down by the side of a mountain, and you wonder at the lives led there.

On the second evening we came into Utah, & the Great Salt Lake and the Salt Lake Desert. The train headed straight out across the Lake on a low wooden causeway which trembled beneath us. When you looked out of the window, you could see nothing at the side or ahead of you but water, and it's like heading out to sea on a train, unnerving, but at least I thought you could float in this salty water... The causeway is 32 miles long, and the train moves very slowly across this lake that covers 2000 square miles. A couple of hours later we were travelling through Nevada, wild, fierce, territory, along the sides of mountain ranges and through canyons that rose sheer and high on either side, utterly dwarfing the train—and there was a huge pale yellow moon a-shining—yes, sirree!!

I'm having an exciting time, but I miss you.
PLEASE WRITE!!"

Shirley

6

Hastings—The War Years

B Y THE TIME DOLLY AND I WERE BORN (1933 AND 1935) GRAN
and Granddad had retired and moved to Hastings. They
lived in a terraced house with a long back garden in Athelstan Road, surrounded by streets with Saxon names such as
Githa, Offa, Alfred, Edmund and Ethelburga.

How we loved the pungent smell of tomatoes in Granddad's
greenhouse, and the tang of tarry rope and woodshavings in
his shed where he made wooden toys for us; and the warmth
of their front step where Granny would sit us down to shuck
peas or string runner beans fresh from the garden. Gran
had an oil lamp bracketed on to her hall wall which gave off a
soft glow and a smoky smell. I loved both—they represented
security. Often clinging to the wall were huge crickets from
the garden. I found them fascinating but frightening and
walked by them very carefully.

My father was a milk roundsman for a local farmer before the war. This was a good job as Dad brought home lots of fresh milk and eggs from the farm, and his employer was a decent man. Occasionally at weekends, he'd lend Dad his car, a black Renault saloon, and we'd drive out to the Downs with Gran and Granddad, all of us piled into the leather-scented luxury. I still associate that smell with my early childhood, and can get very nostalgic at the sight of a car with running boards. As Dolly and I drowsed in the car at the end of a day out, Dad would tell us that he'd drive the car up the twelve front steps when we got home, to save us the bother of climbing them or of Mum and Dad having to carry us indoors, and since I always woke up in my bed the next morning with no recollection of getting out of the car, I believed it.

I also thought my Dad could blow cigarette smoke out of his ears and he could certainly make white rabbits out of handkerchiefs. He spent most of the War years away serving in the Royal Artillery, coming home only rarely on leave. In

A picnic in Sussex, 1936.

1940 our home in Emmanuel Road was hit by an incendiary bomb. Thankfully, Mum had taken us out for our customary walk on the West Hill that afternoon, and she got back to find the house next door completely destroyed, and only half of ours left standing. Dolly and I were evacuated twice, the first time with our school to Welwyn Garden City, while Mum, along with the rest of the mothers, was sent to Somerset. Was it all done for the best by the authorities, this breaking up of families? But off we went obediently on the train with our gas masks over our shoulders, those gas masks that were such a struggle to get over your face, our name-labels pinned to our coats, and our few clothes. I have a vague memory of travelling over a viaduct that seemed enormously high to me, an image of the steps of the house we went to, and of Dolly and me being taken out to the school playground in our wellington boots one morning to have our photograph taken to send to Mum. After six weeks it was decided to re-unite children with their mothers and evacuate the families to Wales.

1937 – on the Sussex Downs, clockwise, Granddad, Gran, Mum, Dolly and me.

Me and Dolly, two evacuees in Welwyn Garden City.

We were sent to Llanelli where Dolly and I amused ourselves by speaking gibberish to each other, pretending to be
princesses from somewhere unnamed but exotic, hoping to
impress the local kids. I recall too how Welsh iced lollies lost
their flavour after just one suck, but as we hadn't had ice-
cream for what seemed an eternity, they still were a great

treat. The nearest town was Velinvoel, which Mum promptly christened Feeling Foul. We were homesick and were glad when some four months later it was deemed safe for us to return to Hastings. As we had no home of our own now, we moved into 27 Canute Road with Aunt Grace and Uncle Cyril, who was a fireman, and their two little daughters, Bridget and Lesley.

The South Coast was hardly a haven though. We faced the German hit-and-run raids, watched dog fights over the Channel, and once when Dolly and I were pushing our baby cousin down Canute Road in her pram, we were strafed by a low-flying plane intent on inflicting as much damage as it could before heading back to the French coast. We had been well taught by Mum to hurl ourselves under hedges at the first sight or sound of a plane. As the days wore on, and we came to no harm, we'd wave encouragement to *our* planes, and I can still recall the thrill of terror when one day we'd rushed out to wave to a low-flying plane, saw the German black cross under its wings, and had to dive for cover. As the War progressed, we learned to tell the difference between the sound of "theirs" and "ours".

7

California to New York

I've been wandering early
I've been wandering late
From New York City
To the Golden Gate

WE WERE IN CALIFORNIA FOR THE BERKELEY FOLK FESTIVAL, appearing alongside Pete Seeger, Jesse Fuller and Sam Hinton, who could whistle and sing at the same time—he performed "Frère Jacques" as a round on his own. It was also our first meeting with the singer Jimmy Driftwood from the Ozarks, a former teacher with an impeccable background of traditional song, coming from both a region and a family where singing was still an essential part of everyday life. Alan thought he was as important a song writer as Woody Guthrie, although not politically driven. His song "The Battle of New Orleans" had been number 1 in the American Hit Parade for

Jimmy Driftwood

ten weeks at the time we met. His voice had a soft rasp to it, a wide Arkansas accent, and the readiest laugh. He was friendly and funny and I loved both him and his music. He dressed in buckskins, with a fringed jacket and a wide hat, and he enthralled his audiences with a most unusual instrument, a mouth bow or picking bow. This was like a hunting bow; but he twanged the string and shaped the notes with his mouth against the wood. He was compelling to watch and to listen to. We became firm friends and he invited us to visit his family in Arkansas when we went South on our recording trip. When we parted in Berkeley, Jimmy kissed me sweetly and sedately on the cheek, saying he loved me like I was his wedded sister! What *did* that mean?

During the festival, Alan upset a few young city-born singers—he called them city-billies—by suggesting that they should learn folk-song *style* at the same time they learned the words and music. It was excellent advice, but they resented it. I thought *they* were arrogant—they thought *he* was. Impasse.

Life seemed very easy in California, too easy, and it irked me. This was odd, since I'd come from the austerity of post-War England, and I could have simply indulged in the luxury of life there. I also felt a bit churlish about these feelings, as we had lovely accommodation, a swimming pool, and sunshine. There was a fad at the time for setting salads and fruit in green jello, rendering the food uniformly tasteless, and without any texture other than slippery. In a way, to me that represented life there. Nothing seemed quite real, nothing had bite or zest. There was little that was robust about urban Californians, they were just too bland—extremely and instantly friendly, but insubstantial, and I couldn't help but

My postcard home from San Francisco.

wonder what the pioneers would have made of it all. But perhaps an easy life *is* what you'd want for your descendants
when you've died in your hundreds, suffered dreadful priva-
tions and crossed hostile territory on foot or in wagons. And
who was I to talk; I hadn't despised myself for travelling there
comfortably by train.

From California we flew back to Chicago. It was the first
time I had flown, and in my letter home I wrote in capitals
that it was A JET—A BOEING 707! It was an inauspicious start
to my flying career. We sat on the runway waiting to take off
at 8.30 am. At 9 the pilot announced there was a fault and at
9.30 we were taken off the plane. At 10.15 we boarded again,
but we still couldn't fly as something had short-circuited. At
10.45 the pilot announced an oil-leak—he was sounding a
little stressed himself by now. I had lost confidence in the
whole venture, short-circuits and oil leaks sounded more like

a Model-T Ford than a Boeing, and when we did finally take off, I quite feared that we'd fly straight into the Rockies.

It turned out to be a smooth and wonderful flight however, America spread out beneath us like a living map in the clear sunlight. Back we flew across the Rockies, the Sierras, the Red Desert. The seemingly endless mountains and sand and prairies made me keenly aware how very vast this Continent was. There was just one more alarm—as we flew over Chicago, there was a grinding roar that shook the plane. My mother's wartime phrase flashed into my mind—"This is it!"—and I hurriedly started to explain to God why I hadn't been to church for years. Alan prised my fingers from his arm and kindly put an end to my fears by explaining that it was the wheels being let down for us to land. Before long we were back in our beloved Buick, and on the road again.

಄ඊ

I described the next part of the journey in a piece I submitted to *The Observer* newspaper in 1963, but it was rejected for publication.

> When the novelty of driving on the great Turnpikes of
> the States has worn off, when it's no longer fun to toss
> your coins from a moving car into the wire baskets at
> the toll booth, when a stop for coffee and a splash of
> cold water at the only oasis for miles fails to revive you
> and you've almost tired of the twenty-eight flavours of
> Howard Johnson ice-cream, when there is little to see
> but the road racing under the wheels and sky dawdling
> overhead, then it's time to switch onto one of the
> delights of America, the local radio stations.

It's rock-and-roll on the New Jersey Turnpike as you drive past the huge chemical factories, oil refineries and black oily wasteland swamps, the airfields where yellow planes swoop just above your car roof. In rural Pennsylvania where the huge barns are painted with good luck symbols you'll hear German accordion bands.

Driving at night into Gary, the Indiana steel town, is almost like entering hell. The road curves in wide sweep, then straightens into the inferno—the sky red with fire, flames leaping from the tall chimneys, billowing clouds of thick orange-tinted smoke, while the radio plays low-down rock-and-roll, the raucous and relentless sound of industrial America.

The most popular station through the South and Mid-West is WCKY, transmitted from Cincinnati, Ohio—"Station Double-Ya-C-K-Whah!—your best station for good-ol'-down-t'-earth-country music" beams the announcer Uncle Wayne Raney of the Singing Raney Family. The music he plays, sizzling blue-grass and hillbilly hymns are the requests of his audience in Kentucky, Virginia and Georgia. Between records he sells a variety of goods in his persuasive Kentucky accent.

"Folks! Did I ever tell y'all about the Gypsy Fish Bait? Here's one way to make sure you don't go home empty-handed on a summer afternoon. Just put some of this fish-bait (a secret that a famous gypsy has agreed to share with you) on your line, and the water'll be a-boilin' and a-leapin' with fish!" The voice drops from excited to conspiratorial. "You see neighbours, when you use the gypsy fish-bait, it appeals to the thousands of little smell-organs all over the fish's body, makes it quiver, and that fish'll attack the bait, and I can promise you neighbours, you'll go home with your pail full! Just mail five dollars..."

"Folks, if you need a little more money right now to buy things you want or perhaps pay those extry bills off, just you drop a line to the DIAL Banking Company, D-Ah-A-Eyell and they'll just send you the money straightaway."

My last ole dollar is gone
Yes my last ole dollar is gone
My rent is due and my whiskey bill too
O honey whatever shall I do...?

"Are you thin, run down? What you need is Wate-on, Double Yah-A-T-E—that's Wate-on, to give you that nice firm flesh that you and other people will admire, all over your body, in just two weeks....."

"Now here's a wonderful offer from your favourite good-old-down-t'-earth country-music programme......

"Folks! Here is the most beautiful family bible you ever saw. There are pages in it to record the births and deaths in your family, and as an added attraction, the words of Jesus Christ are printed in red! And if you send for this beautiful offer, you get extry free gifts: a medallion with the cross on one side and the Lord's Prayer on the other. Folks—buy this Bible for twenty, yes just twenty dollars, and these inspiring gifts are yours."

He ends his programme with songs from The Raney Family's *The Heavenly Sunlight Hymnbook*. A favourite song is "Gathering Flowers for Mother's Bouquet".

Undertaker, undertaker, please drive slow
It's mother you are haulin', an' I hate to let her go.

Another much requested song is "Let's Have a Lot
More Religion and a Lot Less Rock-and-Roll". The books
sell at a dollar each, or as an incentive to buy twelve for
ten dollars, you get a photograph of the Raney Family
playing their guitars, banjos, fiddles, harmonicas and
autoharps thrown in free.

We were all so happy there together
In our peaceful little mountain home
But God needed angels up in Heaven
Now they sing around the great white throne.

CRSO

We were heading up through Michigan to a summer camp,
Circle Pines, near Kalamazoo (and yes, we did sing "I got a gal
in Kalamazoo" as we drove along). Alan's daughter Anne was
spending the summer there, and Alan was giving workshops
for a week or so. On the drive up, Alan said how much he
was dreading teaching at a co-operative summer camp—said
he'd forgotten how to co-operate anyway. I silently agreed. As
we drew closer to the camp, his spirits sank further when we
spotted the jolly doggerel on a notice board:

Follow The Signs>>> To Circle Pines!

Anne had already been there for a couple of days, and as we
joined her for our first meal—beef stew with soggy brown

bread and tinned tomatoes, with three stewed plums each for dessert, Alan wilted. We both cheered up though when we were taken to the little wooden cabin near the lake that was to be ours, and we quickly established a routine of lecturing in the morning, spending the afternoon on the water rowing and swimming, and giving informal workshops and concerts in the evening. The children there really enjoyed the music. One little boy said to me on the last day as we were packing the car to leave, "Is Alan Lomack leaving? He can't leave! I love him! I wish he was my Daddy and my Mommy and my sister I love him so much."

We often gave informal sessions for small groups in the woods, and at one of these I got bitten on the thigh by a spider. Within a few hours the back of my leg was red, angry and hard, raised up from the skin like a plate with two puncture marks in the middle. Several injections of anti-histamine followed by cortisone over four days and it started to go down, but it was painful and I was scared. I was going to be very wary indeed of the insect life of America!

Alan was due to play at The Newport Folk Festival three days after we left Circle Pines, and after a drive of 700 miles back to New York, we had just two days to recover before heading North. On the whole, Newport was a great disappointment to me. "Folk" is such a debased and mis-used word, given far too wide an interpretation by some of its worst perpetrators. Whoever it was said, "Folk music? Well, I ain't never heard a *horse* sing," didn't help. The survival of the music for centuries handed down by word of mouth through many generations of illiterate people is an extraordinary testimony to its power and strength. At its best it is music of great beauty, subtlety and insight into the human condition. It also gives ordinary people a chance to speak for themselves, and set things down in a way they think appropriate for them. It's the voice of those who for generations have been despised, abused and neglected, and for their part in keeping the music alive, I feel they should be honoured, and their music shouldn't be appropriated by people who don't understand this.

Among the singers I disliked were Martha Schlamme, who sang in an operatic style, Odetta, who had a magnificent voice but who also sang in a way that I felt was inappropriate for folk songs, Bob Gibson, "a college-boy type" I wrote deprecatingly, and The Kingston Trio, who had all the energy in the world, but maddened me by kidding the pants off folk music all the time. I despised them. The audience loved them!

Here were some fine performers though, Jimmy Driftwood again, Jean Ritchie the great traditional Kentucky mountain singer, Frank Warner, and Earl Scruggs, the five-string banjo picker. Earl came on stage in a maroon coloured jacket, dark grey trousers tucked into cowboy boots, and a cream Stetson on his head. No expression on his face, completely deadpan, he merely raised an eyebrow when he was about to play something next to impossible on his banjo.

On "Flint Hill Special" he started the tune by just turning the pegs with one hand, making them whine, then flew off into the tune. I was on my feet laughing and yelling and cheering for more. I was simply lifted off my seat by the crackling energy and sheer brilliance of the playing. I wrote in a letter: "It filled me with joy. These real old mountaineers have it, all right. Well, he's not so old, around thirty I'd say."

I was all of twenty-three.

CR80

From Newport we drove up to spend a week on holiday with Lee Falk, an old friend of Alan's, who had a summer house on Cape Cod. Lee was the artist whose two comic strip creations, Mandrake the Magician and The Phantom, had made him extremely wealthy. He was spending the summer in his beautiful weatherboard house by the sea with his actress girlfriend and his mother, and I had the distinct impression those two didn't want us there at all. The actress got tipsy every night and attacked us all with her very sharp tongue. As for Lee's mother, well, Alan said she was typical of a certain type of Western woman (they were originally from Missouri), but I never got round to asking him to explain that. She was contrary, bossy and unfriendly. Lee had hired a new cook for the summer, a Haitian woman who spoke nothing but French, and Mrs Falk didn't speak a word of it. Instead of giving the cook her head and allowing her to cook Haitian food, which Alan said was divine, Mrs Falk made her prepare omelettes filled with cottage cheese for breakfast, and hamburgers and beef stews for the rest of the meals. She then grumbled because she had to spend all day in the kitchen showing the cook how.

One day we went fishing on a boat which Lee had hired. We were after tuna, which we could see leaping through the water, but we didn't catch a single one, even though we were out on the ocean for five hours. Late in the afternoon I felt a drag on my line, something heavy. Wildly excited, Alan and I attempted to wind it in, until the Captain came and took over, untangling the line. Yes, I had caught the dead fish that we were using for bait! Remembering this years later, I wonder how I could ever have wanted to catch such a large and beautiful fish, something I wouldn't dream of doing now, but it was a different world then and we had different perceptions.

Ironically, while walking along the beach that same evening, we saw scores of flounders flapping out of the water on the sand, but instead of taking them home to eat, we tried in vain to put them back into the sea. Next day we went swimming in a fresh-water lake which was full of catfish. I'd never seen any before, and was fascinated and captivated by these blue fish with long whiskers, fish that startled you by swimming towards you, so that you were the one that ducked out of the way. We caught lots of those in our fishing nets, but felt so tenderly towards them, we threw them back too. That evening I was telling Mrs Falk about our day. She stopped me short. "I never eat catfish. I don't like cats!" You don't like me, either, I thought. And I don't like you!

Next day, a mist enveloped the Cape which the weather forecasters said would last for days. Alan and I were feeling worn down by the actress and Mrs Falk, so we packed up and headed back to New York, driving through a severe thunderstorm, with torrential rain that threatened to wash our car off the road. We were in our usual impecunious state, and we only had a couple of dollars in loose change to buy supper on the journey. Alan pulled in at a Chinese restaurant, and ordered one portion of Eggs Foo Yung—scrambled eggs with spring onions and prawns—and I was in my usual state of acute embarrassment as he counted out the coins.

New York was like an oven. Alan was getting dispirited and tetchy. We were starting to despair of making the trip South, waiting for funding to come through. Columbia Records, who were still interested in sponsoring the trip to the tune of $2000, had just come up with a proviso that we must take a Union recording engineer with us—otherwise they would withdraw their offer. Alan knew this wouldn't work in the situations that we would find ourselves in, that it could cause anxiety or self-consciousness in the people we would be recording. From his past experience in the field, he knew we wouldn't be keeping Union hours either. Ours was a labour of love. He turned Columbia down.

It was now past the middle of August. Alan went to Neshui and Ahmet Ertegun of Atlantic Records. To our joy, those two heroes came up with an offer to back the entire trip. We packed the car and polished up the Virginia licence plates (Alan had exchanged the old green Ford for a second-hand Buick, and had taken the precaution of buying a car with a Southern registration, one that wouldn't draw too much attention to us once we were in the South). Within days we were on our way.

8

Hastings—Doodlebug Days

LATER, WE LIVED THROUGH THE DOODLEBUG RAIDS, THE unmanned rockets the Germans launched with such deadly effect from France. They were menacing and terrifying and the silence that preceded the hit was the most frightening part of all. Mum and Grace would look at each other and say, "This is it!" At night we slept under the stairs in a cupboard, two or three adults and four children. When I see the space today, I wonder how we all fitted in. Mum and Aunt Grace made up invective songs about Hitler to make us laugh, and I hated him for ruining my eighth birthday. Gran had managed to make a cake from dried egg and Lord knows what else. I was thrilled. Gran called it a Russian cake—a marbled concoction of pink, green and chocolate, not real chocolate but probably gravy browning! There was an Air-Raid warning just as we were all gathered round the cake in the garden that early July afternoon, and we had to run indoors and shelter under the stairs, leaving the cake behind.

When the All-Clear had sounded and we trooped outside again, the cake was swarming with ants, and although the grown-ups tried to rescue it, we couldn't stomach it. The bombs dropped that afternoon hit the little corner shop two streets away, killing the two elderly ladies who owned it, and who still some-how, despite the sugar rationing, had managed to make some sort of fudgy confection, which they sliced thinly and served in blue paper cones. I *hated* the Germans, and felt guiltily but secretly glad that they used German prisoners-of-war as the Indians that got killed in cowboy films, a belief that was widely held in our primary school. And yet, when German prisoners-of-war were sent to work as labourers on surrounding farms, they were befriended by many of the local people. Aunt Grace took in one prisoner, Leo, as a lodger, and he became a friend of the family, and spent much of his free time with Granddad, talking, whittling wood and playing cards. Some evenings, Mum would join Gran and Granddad and Leo in a game of whist or rummy, and Dolly and I would lie sleepily upstairs in the spare bedroom as the cigarette smoke and the murmur of the grown-ups' con-versation drifted up to us.

In civilian life Leo was a carpenter and all he wanted was to get home to his wife and three little children. When the War ended Grace helped him find his family. She badgered the War Office and the Red Cross for months to no avail. Finally, it was The Salvation Army who succeeded in trac-ing his family to a camp in Russia, and they were eventually re-united, except for one daughter who hadn't survived. Leo carved and painted two wooden airplanes for Dolly and me, a Spitfire and a Hurricane. I wish I still had them.

Mum at the dairy.

A huge excitement in our lives was the arrival of the American food parcels which were distributed through the school, and the best item was the packet of sweetened chocolate powder which Mum would let us have a saucerful of in its dried state. How we loved to lick our fingers and dip them into the luscious stuff. It lasted longer that way and probably went further too! There were clothing parcels from the States which we opened with great excitement, and occasionally we were given shoes at school. All the children would line up, have their feet measured, and if there was a pair that fitted you, you'd be given them. No clothing coupons needed, just the right sized feet.

We collected pieces of shrapnel which were swapped avidly with boys after school, we made a few pennies collecting waste paper and jam jars, selling them to a depot on the Fairlight Road, and we'd treat ourselves to "a penn'orth of crackling" at the fish and chip shop in Ore village, the odd bits of batter that fell off the fish as it fried. We often ran errands for neighbours and family but there was one that always made us nervous. Granddad would hand us a shilling wrapped up in a piece of paper, which we were instructed to hand over to the butcher in Ore village in such a way so that no one could see—and it was always stressed, *not* to the lady in the kiosk who took the money for the meat. We'd stand anxiously in the queue at the butcher's, scuffing our shoes through the sawdust which covered the floor, waiting to hand over the money with a whispered, "From Mr Fred Ball of Athelstan Road." It was years before I realised that he was placing an illegal bet on the horses.

It also worried us when Aunt Grace sent us to the tobacconist's for *two* cigarettes, all she could afford, as the understanding owner kept a packet of loose Woodbines behind the counter. The most embarrassing errand of all was being sent by Aunt Grace to the chemist to buy a rubber teat for the baby's bottle. I thought it was *such* a rude word. I also thought breasts were called humps. (And while we're on the subject, later, when I was about twelve or thirteen, I thought bras were pronounced "braes", the word never having been mentioned at home, and used to get giggling fits when the school choir sang "Ye Banks and Braes o' Bonny Doon", much to the bafflement of my friends.)

The beach at Hastings was out of bounds, mined and bar-ricaded with great rolls of barbed wire against invasion, so we spent most of the War out rambling in the countryside as there was less danger from raids there. We were always in a group, Mum and Aunt Grace pushing her toddler and baby in a huge old pram which those two indomitable sisters would lift over stiles, plough through mud and scramble through woods. Grace could make a picnic out of the most meagre rations, and there was plenty to pick from the hedgerows, such as "bread-and-cheese", the fresh young leaves of haw-thorn in the Spring, nectar to suck from clover flowers, and in the Autumn, hazelnuts, sweet chestnuts and blackberries. Although the strain on them must have been dreadful, the two sisters found plenty to laugh at. Once when we were in Blackbrooks Wood, Dolly and I needed to spend a penny. "Go behind those bushes," said Mum and then collapsed in help-less laughter as the bushes got up and moved away—they were camouflaged Canadian soldiers on manoeuvre!

And as if there weren't enough terrors to overcome because of the War, there were those local ones that loomed so large in our little lives. There was "the Witch's Door"—a tiny gothic wooden door set in a very long old brick wall on a dark, curved part of the Fairlight Road. What you had to do was to knock on the door and run for your life! And we always dreaded going along Martineau's Lane, because there, in a field that we had to walk by, lived William the Conqueror. He was a huge bull who always seemed to be grazing in rather a watchful way just inside the hedge, and we'd creep by, our hearts pounding. It wasn't until we were out of range that we'd yell "Silly old Bill the Conk!"

Uncle George in uniform.

The entire family survived the War, Dad taking part in the liberation of the Channel Islands, Uncle Robin serving in Belgium and France, Uncle George in the 8th Army at El Alamein where he kept two hens called Eggwot and Ermyntrude in the turret of his tank. He read *1066 and All That* as an antidote to all the horrors of the Desert Campaign, the worst of which for him was cradling a dying comrade in his arms while trying to contain his guts which had been blown out by a grenade. He has the tattered copy of that book to this day. He was made a Captain, and he returned home deeply tanned, his face engrained with sand. He'd grown a moustache and acquired a cultured accent befitting his rank. How handsome and dashing he looked; how like a gentleman he sounded; how awe-struck I was by this changed Uncle.

9

Virginia

Away and away we're bound for the mountains,
Bound for the mountains, bound for the mountains,
Over the mountains the hills and fountains,
Away to the chase, away, away.

Dear Mum and Dolly,

This letter is coming to you from Virginia. We're out
on our recording trip now. We arrived late in Salem
and decided to camp out at the foot of the Blue Ridge
Mountains. It took hours to get the tent up in the dark,
Alan trying to hammer tent pegs into the very hard
ground and waking up all the local dogs who barked
furiously, me fussing about snakes and spiders. Alan
got very cross, and when he finally crawled in onto
his air mattress it collapsed! However, we slept very
soundly and woke at 8 the next morning to find we had

camped very near to houses and that two huge trucks
had appeared in the field overnight! We're here at Salem
to visit Texas Gladden and her brother Hobart Smith,
a wizard on banjo, guitar and fiddle. All the family
are delighted to meet someone from England—"and a
mighty pretty one too. Our ancestors come from the
old country." The little Virginia country towns are like
nothing I've seen before—one cinema showing films like
"The Ghost of Dragstrip Hollow", "I Was a High-School
Bride" and "The Giant Behemoth". I laugh at the fruit
shop with its sign that says "Fresh Frout"—but the
peaches you buy are gorgeous!

All the folks we record live way back in the Blue
Ridge Mountains, in lonesome hollers, shady groves,
heads of creeks. We drive up and down rough old tracks
to tumble-down wooden shacks, decaying wood and
furniture, and there's always a couple of mangy hound
dogs who race and bark at the car.

Hobart Smith's family put us up one night and we
had real Southern hospitality, a table groaning with
food, and they say apologetically, "Ain't got much to offer
ye." The table is laden with yellow corn-bread, country
ham, scrambled chicken, fried potatoes, apple sauce,
cinnamon apple jelly, home preserved beans, macaroni
cheese, sweet country butter, salad, peaches, grape
jelly—all utterly delicious. They make you eat enough
for ten, and keep apologising because there isn't more...

It had taken us three days to reach Virginia. We had left
New York at 4 on the Friday afternoon, heading for Washington, where we had to collect the tape recorder. It was an

uncomfortably hot drive down through the smoky, oily air of industrial New Jersey, and a relief to cross the northern tip of Delaware and into Maryland. In those days it was a normal and friendly custom in the States to pick up hitch-hikers, and we gave a ride to a young black man who was on his way to Richmond, Virginia, to look for work. When we told him the purpose of our trip he whooped for joy and said *he* was what *we* needed, *we* were what *he* needed! He sang some spirituals for us, but his voice was coarsened from too much booze and smoking. To make room for him in front I had shifted into the middle seat, with my feet on the gearbox, and they were burning hot. When I complained, Alan realised he'd been driving in first gear for some twenty miles.

We dropped our hitchhiker in Washington and drove to the studios to collect our recorder, only to be told that it still needed some adjusting and wouldn't be ready till the next morning. It was frustrating, but a delicious seafood dinner in an air-conditioned riverside restaurant cheered us. It took all the next day to sort out our equipment, and it wasn't until late afternoon that we headed out for the port of Norfolk where Alan was hoping to find some longshoremen who still sang shanties. We arrived after dark, and Alan drove straight to the black section of town. He parked the car on the street outside a pool hall, told me to stay in the car, and went inside. The street was crowded, and there wasn't a white person in sight. I felt very conspicuous and uneasy, and was relieved when Alan reappeared after an hour, having had no success, but reporting back that this was reputed to be the toughest locality in town, where everyone carried a gun or a knife!

On the Sunday we went to Suffolk, where Alan had arranged to meet James Porter, a black promoter who was to take us to some black churches. Once again, Alan left me inside the car while he went into James's house. I was starting to resent this, and hoped there was going to be more to field recording than sitting in a hot car. When I wound the windows down, wasps and black hornets flew in, but eventually I was rescued by Mrs Porter, who invited me into her cool kitchen and gave me fresh lemonade, apologising profusely for not having invited me in sooner, as Alan hadn't told her I was there.

We then set out with James to a local Baptist church where I was taken aback to see a woman sitting in the porch charging a dollar admission fee. The members of the congregation were very well dressed, especially the Reverend in a dark suit and pristine white shirt. He was none too friendly—but why should he have been? He hadn't invited us, didn't want us recording in his church and he turned us away. From there

Alan recording in Virginia.

James took us to Belleville where he knew of a remarkable *a capella* choir at the Church of the Saints. The church was in an isolated setting, with only one house close by, the home of the deacon. We asked a woman working in the garden if he was at home. Not looking up she replied that he was away. Nobody was welcoming us; I could understand why people would be wary of white strangers, even though we were accompanied by a black man, but it was dispiriting.

We drove to another deacon's home, a large wooden two-storeyed house that was in a state of disrepair and decay, with ragged curtains at the windows. A housekeeper with a child at her skirts let us in, and the deacon greeted us cordially. Inside the house it was pleasant, clean and cool, and the deacon and Alan settled down to a long conversation. Gently our host pointed out that their Sabbath was held on a Saturday, and we had arrived on Sunday, but an arrangement was made that we should go back in October on our return journey north. The day was wearing on and we didn't seem to be getting anywhere. James offered to take us to a Pentecostal Holiness Church that evening. We gratefully took a couple of hours off to swim in the warm but soothing waters of Pine Lake.

The church was a small one on the outskirts of Suffolk, and the Reverend greeted us warmly when we arrived in good time before the service to set up our equipment. Everyone we met that night was friendly and welcoming and it lifted our spirits. One of their members, an old lady, had died a few days back, and her coffin was lying open in the church so that people could pay their last respects. One of the women who had taken me under her wing asked me if I would like to pay mine. I said that I would be honoured. It was the first corpse I had ever seen, and I was surprised at how moved I was. She was so very tiny and nestled in white ruffles. It was touching, too, watching every person who entered the church come to say goodbye, not mournfully, but quite cheerfully.

It was the first time also that I had attended a black church and seen a preacher in action. He was a handsome man, leaping around, clapping his hands to emphasise his words, and to my surprise and initial embarrassment, clutching his crotch frequently. I was fascinated by the whole proceedings, although Alan said the singing wasn't really very good, and the preacher hadn't really set the congregation on fire. The children there were delightful, especially when it was their turn to sing. Four little girls, one aged four, one five, and two six year olds stood behind a table and sang a spiritual, the youngest one supplying the syncopation by singing "uh-huh" between the lines. You could see four pairs of legs under the table, three heads and one big red bow above it. When we played this recording back, everyone laughed and clapped and almost fell over with pleasure. As the evening ended, I asked the lady who had befriended me if there was a lavatory.

"Well, there is," she said, "Outside—but it's full of those big red wasps and people keep complaining of getting stung." I held on.

The machine was "wowing" and we had to get it seen to by an engineer in the CBS station in Norfolk the next day. While it was being fixed, we went into the studios of radio station WRAP to meet Jack Holmes, a black radio announcer and disc jockey—a rare thing then—with a voice of rich warmth. He told us how he got his first job at Station WLOW, twelve years ago. "The American Tobacco Company wanted a man to sell Sweet Pete Snuff. Tried out fifteen to twenty college fellows," he recalled. "When they heard my voice they grabbed me. Sweet Pete is on the market still all over the South. But they didn't announce me as a Negro."

When the truth came out, he had to travel to work in a police patrol car, as there were threats to blow up the station if it continued to employ him. But he was too important to the Tobacco Company to be fired. "Anyway," he said, "things got better after Ed Murrow [the famous American broadcaster] visited the radio station. Oh yes, he squared it away. At first I had fifteen minutes, then thirty, then one hour. Now I do six hours—have done for the last ten years. Nowadays, I got white folks that invite me home to dinner." The young white engineer in the studio obviously adored him, and hung on every word he said. But Jack was still the exception back in 1959.

We wandered round the town and came across a street musician who told us his name was "Tin Cup Shine". He was a one-armed man with skin so dark it had a blue sheen, gap-teeth, grey bristles on his cheeks and chin. He had a shining rail frame strung with hand-carved primitive wooden puppets, people and animals painted red and white, that danced when he pumped the foot pedal, and with his one hand he played a drum. On the back of the rail hung dull silvery frying pans and saucepans. It was a strange and remarkable sight. Alan said that he'd seen something like it before, that he thought it was called a "black cat", that it was magical, probably voodoo. We dropped coins into the collecting tin wishing ourselves good luck for our trip. That evening we collected our recorder, and headed out of Norfolk across Virginia to Salem.

We spent one more night camping in the field, and in the morning we packed our tent, and went to find Texas Gladden. She had been recorded by Alan and his father in the 1930s and '40s and was generally acknowledged as the greatest ballad singer in the States, with a remarkable repertoire of Anglo-American ballads. She was sixty-four, matriarchal, slender and upright, with pretty white curly hair. She sang unaccompanied in the white "lonesome" mountain style, and she wouldn't sing a song unless, as she said, it did something for her, in much the same way as she wouldn't buy a hat or dress for the same reason. But she said she would sing a song just to get one beautiful note out of it. She was a religious woman, a Mormon, but, intriguingly, seemed to have quite a soft spot for the Devil, at least as he appeared in ballads. At one point when she'd finished singing "The Devil's Nine Questions"—

O you must answer my questions nine
Sing ninety-nine and ninety
Or you're not God's, you're one of mine....

Alan asked if she ever visualised the characters in the songs. "Oh, yes," she replied, "the girl is dressed in a crinoline, very blonde, delicate and soft. The Devil is very swarthy, but not a bad looking guy. He's tall and lanky, has a Roman nose, but he's very good-looking. He has a definite persuasive way about him."

She also believed in witches and maintained quite matter-of-factly that witches lived in the community. She told us that one witch in Salem was said to have caused a river to flood. The town elders believed that if they fasted it would reduce

Me and Texas Gladden in Virginia.

her powers. The witch retaliated and warned one elder that if he left town he wouldn't return alive. He ignored her warning, went away, got peritonitis and nearly died. The elders decided the witch was stronger than they were, so they *paid* her to leave town.

Texas gave us angel food cake with ice-cream for lunch and said that in the afternoon she'd like us all to go over to Bluefield to surprise her brothers Hobart and Preston. So along with her husband Jim we piled into the Buick. The road wound steeply through the mountains, with sheer drops at the side, white crosses marking accident spots. The countryside looked very beautiful in a stormy sky, washed by a heavy rain. Hobe and Preston were delighted to see us, and we were equally happy to meet them. They were solid country men with deep gravelly voices. Preston was reputed to be a great preacher, and Hobe was a wonderful fiddle, banjo, and guitar player. He was a fine energetic singer, too, and I never heard anyone play the piano like he did, producing a racing jangle of sound as his rough farmer's fingers flew over the keys. He had pronounced views on what he considered to be good music, and said vehemently of anyone who had the temerity to ask him to play tunes he didn't like, 'If anyone asks can I play 'Redwing' (a popular tune in the mountains) I plank it down that they don't know a thing about music!' This implacability of Hobe's was underlined by something Texas said about her brother. 'Now Hobe can be sorrier than anybody if he pitifuls them, than any body living—or can hate them harder than anyone.' The minute we arrived at the wooden house, the women rushed into the kitchen to start fixing food while we set up the recording machine. As well as singing and playing, the family loved recounting stories and telling jokes, something they'd inherited from their father King Smith who, they said, was telling jokes on his deathbed.

I grew slightly weary of the hail of stories along the lines of: "My son weighed twelve and a half pounds at birth," said Texas. "Just baptised him and put him to school!" Once she sent her son out to count the sheep. "Counted twelve," he reported back, "But I couldn't count the thirteenth 'cause she run off."

"At a prayer meeting," she told us, "there was a very pale woman sitting in the congregation. 'Sister, have you got salvation?' asked the preacher. 'Well, it's either that or worms,' she replied."

Preston, proud of a song he'd just written about a local murder, showed it to Hobe. "How much d'you think I'll get for it?"

Hobe Smith of
Bluefield, Virginia.

"About twenty years!" said Hobe. After that story was told, Preston asked, quite seriously, "Did you ever hear the song about the man who murdered his wife? I thought that was the prettiest song I ever heard."

We spent a wonderful day, recording, talking and laughing. As it got late, Hobe said, "Well, I guess we've cussed and discussed everything and everyone." They put us up for the night, the women still rushing around anxiously asking,

"D' y'all want anything?"

We recorded all the next day, exhilarated by the quality of the music and songs and the sheer good nature of the Smith family. At the end, we drove Texas and Jim back to Salem, and booked ourselves into a motel for the night—five dollars for two. In the morning the woman who ran the place came

Wade Ward and Alan listening to a playback.

over and spoke to us as we sat outside on the wooden steps drinking coffee.

"See that step on the next cabin—killed a rattler there yesterday. If I were you, I wouldn't go down in the long grass—killed six rattlers there in the last two months."

She asked where we came from and what we were doing, and when Alan explained, told us that her husband was an ex-hillbilly band leader. We asked to meet him, but she dismissed the request with a wave of her hand saying, "Ah no—he's out there somewhere flying swats!" She said of Alan's beard, "Why does he have that thing? I don't mind a moustache, but I wouldn't want my teeth brushed every time I kissed him!" It amused me, but made Alan aware that his beard could draw attention to his "foreignness" when we went further South, and might cause problems. By the time we went into Mississippi, he had shaved it off.

Although in Virginia we were concentrating on white mountain music, we did run into a black gang working on the line at the tiny railroad station under the hills at Elliston, just a few miles away from Salem. Alan asked if they still sang work songs for laying tracks. Their leader Simmons told us with remarkable eloquence: "Well, we kinda used to. Any old rhyme just to liven the work up. Most of them were pretty dirty, but some of 'em didn't sound so bad, but you knew what they meant anyway! You'd get everyone rappin' the rail together and you could jump track that you couldn't lift. Just like one drop of water cain't do nothin', but you get a whole lotta drops of water together and they sweep the earth."

He sang us a track lining song:

Leader: *Alright, boys, is you alright?*
Gang: *'Right! 'Right!*
Leader: *Don't mind workin' from sun to sun*
             But it look like payday never come.

The person I grew fondest of in Virginia was Uncle Wade Ward of Galax. He had first been recorded by the Lomaxes in 1939 for the Library of Congress. His mother was a fine ballad-singer, and his father, Davy Crockett Ward, was a good fiddler. They were both dead now, but Wade, at turned seventy, was still playing his own distinctive, unhurried, rippling banjo. He was of English-Cherokee ancestry, had a sweet gap-toothed smile, a gentle manner and was very softly spoken. I was touched by the story of how he'd re-married after his first wife died. His second wife told us that she was listening to the radio one morning and heard him play "The Carroll County Blues".

'Uncle' Charley Higgins and Wade Ward.

"I've got to meet that man," she said to her sister. A meeting was arranged and Wade, too, felt an immediate response. "It was a second marriage and we was both experienced to what life was, so we didn't have to do a whole lot of courting. I reckon neither of us has ever been sorry." Wade picked up his banjo and looked at her steadily as he played, meaning every note of it. He spoke of his wives as his "first and second Madam".

I was so glad he had someone to take care of him, as I'd worried for a whole day about his health, for as we sat outside on the porch, he occasionally spat out dark blood. Later, when I mentioned my concern to Alan, he laughed and told Wade. Wade chuckled so hard he almost choked on the tobacco plug he'd been "chawin" and spitting out all day long.

We recorded many tunes from him, his life-long friend eighty-one year old Charlie Higgins, whose fiddle was two hundred years old and who'd been playing since he was eight,

Name	Address	Phone No.	Birth-days	Anniver-saries	Christmas	Valentine's Day	Easter	Other Occasions
Texas Gladden & Jim, Rte 3, Box 497, Salem, Va.								
Wade Ward, Independence, Va.								
Charlie Higgins, Rte 2, Galax, Va.								
Estil & Okna Ball, Grassy Creek, N.C.								
Horton Barker, Rte 2, Chilhowie, Va.								
Spencer Moore, Rte 2, Chilhowie, Va.								
Sidney Hemphill, Senatobia, Miss.								
George Fields, Lexington, Ala.								
Connie Odum, St Joseph, Tennessee								
Albert & Emma Hammond, Lexington, Ala.								

CHRISTMAS CARD AND FRIENDSHIP LIST
After a "permanent record" entry here . . .
"remind" yourself on the calendar pages.

My address book entries from Virginia.

and Mister Dale Poe on guitar. The music absolutely delighted us—and them too when they heard it played back through the earphones. "If they don't quit that I'm gonna get up and dance!" Charlie laughed, and when on the playback, he heard Alan ask, "Can you play 'Bonaparte's Retreat'?" he reached for his fiddle to play it again. They had been making music together for the past forty years, playing at auction sales for the Parsons Auction Company. These were often sad events when a family was selling up due to debt or death. Charlie explained, "We kindly entertain the crowd and make it possible so when they get onto a little squabble there, we can help 'em straighten it out by fiddling a little." They said that Charlie could play all day and all night and never play the same tune twice, and I don't think they were exaggerating.

The days in Virginia were very rewarding, both in terms of the people we met and the material we recorded. I loved watching Alan at work, building affection and trust. Recording in the field is a difficult task, but Alan brought to it his years of experience, wide-ranging knowledge, unfailing patience, humour, enthusiasm, judgement and integrity. He could calm a nervous performer with his informal approach or give confidence to an anxious one. He had an infectious chuckle and a down-to-earth friendliness and warmth that charmed people. It was obvious that he loved them and their music, and they responded to him by giving their best. Strangers became friends.

We were heading off towards Kentucky, driving through towns which amused me with their names, such as Cinderella, Cucumber, War, Panther. We had one more Virginian to revisit. This was Estil C. Ball, who lived at Grassy Creek, Rugby, a very fine singer and guitar player, a man the Lomaxes had recorded some twenty years earlier, when he sang the secular songs and ballads of the mountains. But in the intervening years, he had, as he put it, "turned sanctified", and was singing his own compositions, religious songs, in his church and on the local radio station.

He was an impressive figure, with a grave and courteous manner. He was tall and handsome with hair so black I was put in mind of a line in one of my granddad's songs, "The Bonny Labouring Boy"—*his hair is like the raven's wing...* But although the Virginian courtesy was there, the absolute good humour, sweetness and ease of manner of say, Hobe or Wade, was missing. The mood was darker. The language of the songs was full of foreboding, telling of angels of wrath, fire from heaven and blood filling the seas.

It was just a taste of what we were to encounter in Kentucky.

10

Hastings—Substandard

THERE WAS A CASUALTY OF THE WAR—MY PARENTS' MARRIAGE. Their love for each other couldn't overcome the changes that six years separation had wrought. And they *had* been in love. Dad wrote poems to Mum throughout the war, and printed a little book of them when he got home. Mum, who had been working as a tram conductress in Hastings, had grown used to being independent. Dad wanted her to stop work and resume her life as housewife and mother. She refused. Neither could re-adjust to this new life, and eventually Dad left home when I was fourteen, Dolly sixteen. I couldn't understand why the fact that they'd come safely through the War and been re-united wasn't enough to hold them together, why simply being grateful they had survived wasn't enough; but that was a child's perception.

Dad moved in with a red-haired (dyed) widow and her two children who lived just a couple of streets away, and we

Dad during
the War.

would see him out with his new family. I was so distressed
by this that my school work suffered, and in my second form
at Grammar School I had to stay down and do the whole
year over again, adding humiliation to grief. And worse—our
headmistress announced at a morning assembly that Shirley
Collins had the distinction of being the only girl in the history of the Hastings High School to get *no marks at all* for her
algebra exam. Although some girls at school had lost their
fathers in the War, no one else in the school had parents
who were separated—it wasn't the commonplace thing it is
now, and I felt so ashamed. Dad and the widow moved to
Southampton, and I only saw him once again in my life when
I was thirty-two. He sent Dolly and me a Christmas present
one year, a pair of stockings each. They were stamped "Sub-
standard" and I threw mine away unworn.

11

Kentucky

Rattlesnake oh rattlesnake
What makes your teeth so white?
Been lying in the wilderness all my life
And I ain't done nothing but bite

BEFORE I LEFT ENGLAND, I WAS FULL OF ROMANTIC AND NAÏVE ideas about Kentucky. It was a place that had always fascinated me, and the one I most longed to visit, as one of my favourite American traditional singers, Jean Ritchie, was a Kentuckian whose mountain family had a wealth of songs and ballads from generations back. I had a hazy notion that I would be going back in time to a place where the mountaineers still used many old English words, lost to us at home, and I knew from the collecting done by Cecil Sharp and Maud Karpeles in 1916 that traditional song in Kentucky was in a remarkable state of preservation, guarded by people who lived in isolation by choice, and who still clung to a way of life that was precious, even essential to them. I was moved by the fact that the pioneers, leaving harsh conditions in the Old Country, searching for religious or economic freedom, had still kept their songs from home. Was it because they were the one familiar thing in this strange, vast, dangerous and unknown wilderness?

But the truth was that in Kentucky I started to feel afraid. The beauty of the place was undeniable, the mountains high and steep, heavily wooded, greeny-blue deepening to purple at dawn and sunset, when pink clouds nestled down in the hollows or haloed the peaks.

Amidst all the beauty was hardship and deprivation for many mountaineers. We heard of the miners' bitter conflicts with mining companies and their armed guards.

They say in Harlan County
There are no neutrals there
You'll either be a union man
Or a thug for JH Blair

There were also feuds between families and neighbours, reports in the local newspaper of a man killed because his cow strayed into a neighbour's pasture. I lay in bed at night and could hear gun shots in the hills, and didn't know whether the prey was animal or human.

On September 6th, a hot clear day, we went to record Old Regular Baptists at an outdoor prayer meeting on the hillside outside the town of Blackey, the meeting ground five miles off the road and up a dirt track just wide enough to let our big Buick through. Here in the open-air was a large gathering of preachers and worshippers from all over Kentucky, some families with young children, but mostly middle-aged and elderly people, men in their shirt sleeves and women in cotton frocks and hats, some sitting under parasols, some gently fanning themselves, the air filled with the sound of crickets, or katydids as they called them.

The surroundings were pleasantly rural, but before long I started to feel nervous, fearful even. The people stared at us as we arrived and set up our recording equipment. They didn't appear hostile nor very curious, but rather they were watchful and silent, and it was that aspect of it that unnerved me. The Baptists there kept to the old Scottish way of lining the hymns, a method used in the past for people who were illiterate, so that instead of singing a hymn from a book, the congregation would listen to the preacher sing each individual line, and then they'd repeat it.

The voices were harsh, strangled and fervent, the sound swelling and soaring across the hills in a way that thrilled and moved me. *Guide Me O Thou Great Jehovah, Pilgrim through this barren land*, they sang, but this was not the reassuring hymn that we know sung by a Welsh rugby crowd, more a heart-stopping sound of people in torment. Hearing such loneliness and pain resonating through the singing brought home to me again how harsh life must have been for the settlers.

We had man-handled the big Ampex recorder up the hill and on to the meeting ground, plus the mikes and two heavy batteries, and had recorded for an hour or so, when one of the preachers stood up and said, "I've been preaching all my life without the aid of them 'phones. No one asked me if they could be here, and I don't know who's responsible, but I ain't gonna say one single word more till them things is *gone!"* There was a profound silence and all heads turned to look at us. We had no choice but to dismantle "them 'phones" and pack up. As we worked, he started to preach, and turned his sermon against us. He was a Primitive Hard Shell Baptist: he said my 'bobbed' hair was sinful, the machines the work of the Devil. The word "abomination" was used too, and I felt very nervous. Worse was to come. We always carried a tiny portable recorder, a Nagra, a rare object in those days. I believe there were just two proto-types in the world at that time, and we'd been lent one by the Swiss company Nagra to test. Alan passed it surreptitiously to me saying, "We've got to get this down—go and sit under the bank and record it." It was an order. Who was I more scared of, Alan or the preacher?

I crept under the bank, trying to hide the Nagra under my jacket. By now the preacher was well into his stride, he was sobbing and wailing, his voice breaking as he threatened eternal damnation for whoever allowed "them 'phones" to be brought to the meeting ground. So jittery was I that I inad-vertently pressed the play button, and the preacher's voice shrieked out from the recorder. I didn't wait to see if he'd heard—I was only aware of Alan looking rather surprised as I fled down the path and back to the car.

After a while I recovered my nerve and rejoined Alan. The preacher had finished, the crisis was over, and we were allowed to stay and record the rest of the meeting, for as a kinder preacher said, "Why, this young man and his little contraptions might be the means of someone knowing that the songs of Zion are still being sung."

Opposite: The open air meeting in Blackey, Kentucky.

It fascinated me that a great many of the sermons and prayers were full of references to the wilderness, and of the hardships the early settlers endured as they carved, cut and thrashed their way through it. Some even yearned for the old days...

> "When they first stormed the wild seas they lived hard, they had to clear land, they didn't have any houses at all, just rough little log huts—didn't have no chairs like we have now nor no beds to sleep on. But the Lord was with them. Grace divine was with them in such a strong way, that evenings, they would sit on their little dirt porches on three-legged stools in old hog-skin moccasins and coonskin caps...
>
> God was with them and blessed them to have all kinds of good fruit in this land and country, meat and all... and you couldn't hardly hear your ears when you went out in the woods for the acorns and chestnuts and everything a fallin' and rollin' through the timber...
>
> If it had been God's will I'd love to have lived back then, I would... I feel like, that when they left home, goin' to meetin', they sung all the way there, ridin' their horses through the hills... and when they got there, no wonder they shouted, no wonder they rejoiced because they had one thing in mind, that was to honour and to glorify their King."

If you think I'm exaggerating my earlier fear, the texts reproduced on the following pages were printed on a card handed to me by the preacher I ran away from, and see if it doesn't cause you the same unease that I feel, even reading it at forty years' remove and many miles' distance:

THE HEAVENLY FATHER LAW

<u>IS</u>

THOU SHALT NOT DO ANY
UNRIGHTEOUSNESS - UNHOLINESS

THOU SHALT NOT KILL

THOU SHALT NOT EAT ANY
FLESH NOR BLOOD LIFE

THOU SHALT NOT STEAL

THOU SHALT NOT LIE

THOU SHALT BE TRUTHFUL

THOU SHALT NOT COMMIT ADULTERY

THOU SHALT BELIEVE -TO
CONCEIVE IS MARRIAGE

THOU SHALT NOT HAVE EVIL LOVE

THOU SHALT CALL FRUITS MEAT

THOU SHALT NOT CALL FLESH MEAT

THOU SHALT NOT CUT HAIR OFF HEAD ROUND-
ING NOR TRIM BEARD ROUNDING

THOU SHALT NOT WEAR GARMENT OF
DIVERSE COLOR

THOU SHALT NOT DRINK NOR MAKE
STRONG DRINK

THOU SHALT BELIEVE SWEET WINE IS IN
SWEET HOLY FRUITS

THOU SHALT BELIEVE IN MAKING LEVEL SWEET
BEAUTIFUL HOLY LAND HOLINESS

THOU SHALT BELIEVE RUST DOES CORRUPT

THOU SHALT WATCH AS SAME AS PRAY AND
JUDGE RIGHTEOUS. THERE ARE MANY CREA-
TURES; BEES, SERPENTS, DRAGONS, WARRIORS.

<u>YES</u>

READ THE BIBLE HISTORY
<u>THE LAW BOOK</u>

THOU SHALT BELIEVE AND KEEP IN MIND THE EARTH AND ALL FLESH AND BLOOD LIFE IS STILL CORRUPT AND MUCH WORSE THAN IN NOAH'S TIME AND THE HEAVENLY FATHER HAS REASONS TO HAVE GREAT WRATH.

This hard life certainly shaped people's characters. We'd been befriended by a lawyer, a local historian, and he'd arranged for a banjo picker, Ada Coombs, an old mountain woman who lived by herself in a shack up in the hills, to come down to his house so that we could meet her. As we sat on his porch, waiting for Ada, the talk turned to the wildlife of the area—of the increase in rattlesnakes and copperheads in the nearby woods. I was fascinated by and totally attentive to this conversation and kept my feet up off the porch floor for the rest of the evening.

Ada didn't turn up that night, so the following morning we asked for directions to her place and set off hoping to find her at home. She lived a couple of miles off the road—you could drive the first mile up the track and then you had to walk. I refused to get out of the car at that point—the signpost said "RATTLESNAKE CREEK". Alan pulled his socks up over his trouser ends and walked resolutely away and I sat in the car anxiously for nearly two hours.

It was a great relief to see two figures coming back down the track. Ada, eighty-six years old, was wearing her best

Ada Coombs on her porch, Whitesburg, Kentucky, September 1959.

dress—a black lace number (in fact her only dress, she said, she usually wore jeans), her purse thrust into her bosom, a large glittering brooch and dangly earrings, bright red sandals and brilliantly varnished finger and toe nails. The old wooden banjo she carried was bedecked with purple ribbons. She said she'd been too busy hunting squirrels the previous night to get down to see us, and in any case, she didn't feel too good because she'd been stung by a hornet, and her hand had "swolled up" and was too stiff to play the banjo.

Later, back at the lawyer's house, she played for us, but her hands were shaking badly, and she couldn't remember a song all the way through. She entertained us instead with stories of her family, how her Grandfather had settled in the hills in 1842. During the Civil War he had hidden his land deeds in a hollow tree, along with his fiddle that had been brought "across the waters" by his forebears from England. He'd done

Ada Coombs playing banjo for local children on her porch.

this to keep them safe from marauding gangs—Jayhawkers as they were called.

Ada was a fine shot with her double-barrelled shotgun. "I shoot squirrels 'n' rabbits—shot a woman once, too. My husband brought her home, so I shot her in the ankle so she shouldn't come in." She was arrested and sent to jail for a while, and given a longer sentence because she shot the woman on a Sunday. She'd lived in the same cabin in the hills all her life, alone now since her children left home and her husband had died. She'd been to a big town just once "to see a circus—saw a rattler as big round as a horse and a hog as big as two horses". (What were these creatures—a boa-constrictor and a hippopotamus?) She told us about the times she'd been to the Snake Handlers' meetings, a religious sect in Kentucky that believe they are given Divine protection

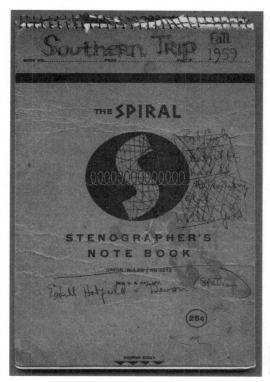

Cover of one of my original notebooks from the 1959 collecting trip.

when handling poisonous snakes. "Yes," said Ada, "they'd pick up the rattlers and they'd bite 'em and kill 'em."

"What!" I exclaimed, aghast—"They'd bite and kill *snakes?*"

"Lord no, honey—the snakes'd kill *them!* I told them I'd take my gun and kill ever' one of them if I ever went thar agin." Alan wanted to go and find the Snake Handlers, but I said, "No."

And I meant it.

Ada left us a present of a dead squirrel to make a stew, and our lawyer friend volunteered to cook it for us provided we had four days to spare as he thought it would take that long to get it tender.

We were heading for Tennessee next, gladly leaving behind the snakes and the hornets, the dangerously steep and narrow mountain roads, the moonshine and gunmen up in the woods. We drove through the Cumberland Gap where the flatlands lay before us, such a beautiful and fertile valley that I wondered why the Kentuckians had chosen to stay in the tangled wilderness of the mountains.

Dear Mum and Dolly,

My romantic illusions about Kentucky have fled like pigeons from a cat. The prettiest sight I've seen in the whole journey is the Cumberland Gap. As we drove through, the sky was quite pink, patched with blue, and the clouds were like trails of pink cotton wool wrapped around the mountains. And as we crossed into Tennessee, with the valley and flatlands before us, the sky turned orange and yellow and palest green, and changed every second. It was unbelievably beautiful.

The people in Kentucky.....well, I was nervous the whole time we were there. These people are primitive, backwoods....Even in the towns. There's just as much shooting and killing as ever there was. And they were in the middle of a coal grievance where we were, some private mines trying to keep open, but paying their men much less than the union mines, and the unions were trying to close them. So the private mines were being guarded by men with guns, Kentuckians who shoot first and ask questions later; who drink moonshine that really is evil stuff, and makes men evil. While we were there two men were killed, about three miles from where we were recording; and a gun battle in the woods all night. Men lying up in the woods waiting to pick people off like they do rabbits. And because so many wild animals are being killed off, the snakes are on the increase, rattlesnakes and even deadlier copperheads. In one place it was so bad that state troopers out searching for a lost youth had to turn back because there were so many!

We'd seen some of these Japanese hornets, like the one that stung Ada, back in Galax, Virginia. They've only been around for the last three years or so, no one knows how they got here. All they know is that they are terrifying and that the sting can be fatal. Six people died in Galax this summer, and the lady we stayed with there, a doctor's widow, not given to tall stories, said she was stung by one, intended to get straight to hospital but couldn't drive because it paralysed her. Luckily a neighbour heard her call, and she got an injection in time. The reason Ada didn't die I imagine is that her blood is probably more poisonous than the hornet's! We saw a couple of the things—they always fly in pairs— and they are terrifying. Easily twice the size of a large bumblebee, they look like GIANT wasps, with large stingers on the end. One had flown onto Ada's hand, and she said, 'I just picked hit off and it stung me!' She sounded so surprised!

Shirley

12

Hastings 1947—Home Life

MUM HAD FOUND A HOUSE TO RENT TWO DOORS FROM GRAN and Granddad, and they helped look after us girls while Mum worked shifts on the Hastings trams. Our grand-parents lived at 121 Athelstan Road, a house we loved to visit. 117 Athelstan Road had an outside lavatory in the back yard which led into the back alley and then to the long garden, and I was scared to go to the lav after dark. There was no electric light so you never knew for sure if a spider or a murderer or a ghost was lurking. There were no loo rolls—we used torn up newspaper threaded on string which hung from a nail on the wall. I was very impressed once when I was invited to tea at a school friend's house. They had an indoor lavatory *and* proper toilet paper, but then her dad *was* a civil servant.

The garden was very productive and we grew all our own fruit and vegetables. I had won a prize at primary school for my "Dig For Victory" poster during the War, so felt obliged to pull my weight, but my least favourite jobs were picking cat-erpillars off the cabbages and dropping them into a bucket of salt water, and cutting the grass with hand shears. What blisters! And what hard work house-keeping must have been for Mum.

There was a scullery complete with a copper and mangle where the wash was done on Mondays, with no hot water on tap. The tin bath was taken down from its hook on the wall every Friday evening and filled with hot water which was boiled up in the copper, for our weekly bath—Dad first (while he was still there), then Dolly, then me and finally Mum, and that bath water was pretty grey and scummy by then. We helped with the housework to some extent. Stand-ing on chairs at the scullery sink, we played at washing up until the water got cold, and we quite enjoyed scattering used tea-leaves over the carpet and brushing them up—this was the favoured way of getting the dust up in the days before vacuum cleaners were common—and scrubbing the pine table with Vim, the bleach powder, until our fingers grew white and wrinkly.

Our playground was the street. We'd stretch our rope right across the road and skip for hours, we'd play hopscotch, whips and tops, or simply throw a netball or a rounders ball to each other, which we loved, and because we were so prac-tised we were both in our school teams. The memory of taking a rounders catch stays with me, that simple satisfaction of a ball falling into your hand from the air. We made slides on the icy pavements in the winter, much to the anxiety of our more elderly neighbours, we burst tar bubbles in the gutter in the heat of summer, and improved our tennis strokes no end by hitting balls up against the enormous flat back wall of the Victorian Anglo-Catholic church at the bottom of the road. Its stained glass windows were very high up, and at no risk from us. And when we tired of the street, there were plenty of trees to climb at the top of the garden and apples to scrump from the orchard over a neighbour's wall.

There were no cars. We had occasionally to get off the road if Percy Lindridge the milkman, whose dairy was a few houses up from ours, came by in his horse and cart. One of my favourite tasks was taking the jug to the cart for the milk and watching Percy ladle the milk straight from the churn into the jug with never a drop spilled. Or we'd run indoors to tell Mum or Gran if the fishman came up with his handcart which he'd pushed all the way up from the beach at the Old Town with his load of freshly caught dabs.

If there were some spare pennies, Mum would treat us all to a pint of shrimps. We'd sit round the table and eat them out of a large bowl with another at the side to put the shells in, and it's still one of life's little mysteries how the pile of shells was bigger than the original pile of shrimps. In the summer, farmers would bring in their handcarts laden with plums and cherries, big white Napoleons, and a regular visitor throughout the year was the rag-and-bone man.

"Ragg-a-bo!" You could hear his cry from streets away, but of course in those days there were few other sounds to hide it. One very wet and bitterly cold winter day Mum took pity on the rag-and-bone man, and asked him in to have a cup of tea and sit by the kitchen range to warm up. "Thank you, Mum," he said with great dignity as he left. "I shall never forget your appreciation." The other visitor we always welcomed was the gas meter collector, because, after he'd counted the pennies that were in the meter, there was always a small refund, a little pile of pennies that he pushed across the kitchen table to you—and we were in funds again!

All the neighbours got on well, the Stubberfields, who let us borrow their dog Jim to take for walks, the Joneses who drank and fought, but not violently so. Mr Jones occasionally chased Mrs Jones out of her house—and her preferred route was straight along Gran's corridor, through the scullery and out the back door, with Mr Jones, who was rather more stout than his wife, lumbering after. No doors were locked in those days, and in the summer, left wide open. But Granddad used to get a bit irritable with this invasion by the Joneses and he'd tell Gran to "close the bloody door for Christ's sake so we can get some peace!"

Dolly and I were chased by another neighbour, the son of the family who lived immediately next door to us. Colin who wasn't "all there" in the parlance of the time, was just a couple of years older than us, and used to chase us the length of Athelstan Road, right round the tops of the gardens and back. So what? So he was flourishing his Dad's axe—that's what! Dolly and I could outrun and outwit him and we'd always get home first and run and hide in Gran and Granddad's. But why did anyone think this was allowable or acceptable? His Dad kept two horses in a field at Fairlight, a ten-minute walk away, and Dolly and I were allowed to ride them. Dolly was, as always, fearless. I was a bit scared, but liked riding once I was up on a horse; it was being down at their restless hooves that bothered me.

One day in the field, which was surrounded by a ten-foot high thickset thorn hedge, Dolly took it into her head to try to ride Jacko bare-back. Jacko, not known for the sweetness of his temper, obviously had other ideas, and was growing very irritable. Dolly was set upon her ride, but I started to make my escape by creeping towards the hedge which was seventy or so yards away. Jacko spotted me and started towards me. I fled—and the next thing I knew, I found myself in the lane on the other side of this impenetrable hedge, completely unscathed, not a scratch. There wasn't a gap in the hedge, nothing. It was as if I had simply materialised on the other side. It was the first time I had seen Jacko look nonplussed.

13

In Search of the
Memphis Jug Band—1959

ONE OF MY FAVOURITE BLACK AMERICAN SOUNDS WAS THAT OF the old jug bands that were so popular in the 1920s and '30s. Several had made commercial recordings: The Cincinnati Jug Band, Cannon's Jug Stompers, and The Memphis Jug Band. There was a gentle drive to the music enhanced by the soft whoomping made by blowing across the mouth of a whiskey jug. As we were in Memphis, we thought we'd try to find out if any of the original Memphis Jug Band members were still alive and playing. It was a long shot, but during his various visits to the clubs Alan had made enquiries, and one guitar player said he knew of their whereabouts, that they were still playing, and he knew their leader, Son Hibler. A meeting was arranged, we met Son and went off with him one drizzly evening to meet his band. I wrote it up at the time:

> We followed Son Hibler through the courtyard of the tenement building, picking our way gingerly through the mud and puddles that were tinged yellow from the dim lights. We walked up two flights of stairs and along a poorly-lit corridor, where from behind closed doors came sounds of domestic quarrels and loud music from radios.
>
> Son knocked on the door of number 7 and we walked into a room where the walls were pasted with brown paper, and red cracked lino lifted off the floor. There were several broken clocks, all stopped at different times, calendars that were years out of date with pin-ups from the forties, and a printed religious text between them: "The Gift of God is Eternal Life." There were two whiskey ads and two sepia photographs, one of a very old black woman staring frozenly straight ahead, and the other of a toddler, bewildered and tearful, collared up to the chin and cuffed down to the wrists. Several pairs of broken spectacles lay on the table, and a drunken man, grumbling in his sleep, lay across the quilt on the large iron bedstead.
>
> There were three women in the room. One of them, in her forties, wearing a black dress with lacy frills, large gold earrings and gold slippers, stood shaking her head affectionately at the man on the bed, and as she smiled, three knife-cut scars deepened in her cheek. The second woman grinned at him too, and took another drink from a whiskey bottle. She wore red

Memphis Jug Band

Throu gh a rain-puddled, muddy, stone-flagged courtyard, in at the
door of the tenement, up the stairs and along a dimly-lit corridor
we followed Son Hibler. Sounds of quarreling came from behind many
of the doors. *We went in* At the seventh identical door, peeling brown paint,
~~nextxxxxx The Walls~~ *Plain brown paper covered the walls,* ~~of the room were papered with brown paper,~~ and
the old red linoleum was cracking and lifting on the floor. There
were several clocks, registering for ever one thing – the time they
stopped; there were old calendars on the walls, with pin-up girls
wearing the square-shouldered dresses of wartime; kitchen cloths
protected the tables, a slogan protected the family –'The Gift of
God is .Eternal Life.' For pictures, there were whiskey ads; and two
old ~~photographs,~~ *sepia prints,* one of a very old Negro woman staring straight ahead,
and the other of a baby, bewildered and tearful, collared up to the
chin, cuffed down to the wrists. Several pairs of ~~glasses~~ *spectacles* lay
around, some for a one-eyed man. On the large iron bedstead hung a
padlock, and a drunken man ~~lxxx~~ lay across the quilt, grumbling in
his sleep.

I sat in an easy chair, and alittle more of the yellow. filling
crept out. The one good chair was in the tiny kitchen, a whiskey
bottle set down beside it. The stove was black with grease; the fish
lying by it were fresh from theriver.

Three women were in the room. One of them, forty years old,
wearing a black dress with lacy frills, golden earrings and slippers,
belonged, for that night at least, to the man on the bed; she *shook her head* ~~smiled~~
as he grumbled, and ~~xhookxhatxhead~~ *smiled*; the three knife scars on her
cheeks deepened. The second wore red ~~shorts~~ Bermuda shorts and a
cream blouse, opened down to her flat, pendant breasts. She grinned
at the drunken man, for she ßs drunk, too. The third, an old woman,
~~lxxxxxx~~left as we came in.

Two of the band were there, one blowing a whiskey jug, the
other tuning a ~~guitar~~ banjo. They nodded, accepted a cigarette, and
went back to their music. Three more musicians arrived middle-aged
and friendly, and finally a handsome, sulky young ªegro, carrying an
electric guitar. 'He plays clubs,' said Son proudly. The man barely

The original draft from my diary describing my meeting with the Memphis Jug Band.

Bermuda shorts and a cream blouse open down below her flat pendulous breasts. The third walked out as we came in.

I was shown the easy chair to sit on, one arm broken and its filling leaking out. There was one other chair, a wooden one in the kitchen, a whiskey bottle set down beside it. The stove was black with grease, but the fish lying in a basket by it appeared to be fresh from the river.

Two of the band were already there, one blowing into a jug, the other tuning his banjo. They coolly nodded a greeting to us, accepted cigarettes, then turned back to their instruments. Soon, three more musicians arrived, elderly and friendly, and finally a handsome sulky young man carrying a flashy electric guitar. "He plays clubs," said Son proudly. The young man barely acknowledged us, but took out his guitar and tuned up. While the others started arguing over which songs to play, the old woman burst back into the room, followed by two tall young men. She had changed her clothes and was now wearing a white blouse, thigh-length blue skirt, and thick stockings rolled down to her knees. She started to dance, flirting with the men with her old reddened eyes, a saucy bow bobbing at the back of her head.

The rehearsal started. While the band played rustily through some forties dance tunes, one of the young latecomers, his hat tipped over his eyes, cigarette hanging from his lips and his eyes narrowed against the smoke, danced with the younger woman, his large hands around her back, his thumbs playing over her breasts. His friend took two spoons out of his pocket and cracked them in time to the music against his thighs, his shoes, the door, the table and the girl's buttocks, his one good eye gleaming with devilment, his yellow-clouded eye rolling. He laughed showing teeth that were long and misshapen, then he picked up the whiskey bottle and played that, too, rolling it around in his hands, dancing, his hips tipping and shaking.

Son and one of his friends, Joe, both of whom claimed to be the original founder of The Memphis Jug Band, started to quarrel passionately, shouting into each other's faces....

"You play your songs! I'll play mine! I'll make the money on mine!"

"All right then! I made the Memphis Jug Band. I'm the leader! The tunes are mine!"

Joe got his song going first, a lively tune he sang with great verve, a wide malicious smile and a crazy laugh. Son's songs were melancholy and Joe teased him. Son grew resentful, but with a show of weary indifference, he joined in. The guitarist who "played clubs" was bored and looked at his watch every five minutes. The bass player whose deadpan expression hadn't changed since we arrived, suddenly came to life as he started to sing "I cooked her breakfast, brought it to her myself! Well, what else could I do boy!" and his wild laughter was echoed by the kazoo player. Another man bent over his jug and blew lugubriously into it, but there was none of the deep resonant tuneful whoomph that was there on the early recordings, and none of the gently rocking, melodious and sweetly harmonised songs either.

The woman in black, tired of dancing, peered at her reflection in a cracked mirror through a pile of hats— pork pies and trilbies—that the musicians had stacked against the glass. From one of the calendars, Lucille Ball and Desi Arnaz grinned, a cockroach crawling over and over them. As the woman moved away, she knocked over a fairground doll that was propped against a bottle of alcohol compound. She left it on the floor where it had rolled against a pile of fish bones, and picked her way with drunken care across to the open window, caressing the man still asleep on the bed as she passed.

Towering way across the city, The Peabody Hotel, a white skyscraper hung with jewelled windows of blue, cream and palest sea-green, proclaimed itself in neon in the dark night sky.

14

Post-War Hastings—1948

AFTER THE WAR, WHEN THE BARRICADES WERE FINALLY removed from the beaches, the seaside was our favourite playground, the knee-grazing and toe-scraping rocky pools at Rock-a-Nore full of fascinating sea life. The Hastings Old Town fishermen offered rides out on their fishing smacks, and you had to walk a plank to get aboard, a big rough sun-burned hand at the end to help you on to the deck. How wonderfully secure that felt.

Once back on the beach, another fisherman, Biddy the Tubman, was there to entertain. He wore a white vest and a top hat, and whirled himself around on the waves in a half-barrel, standing balancing on the rim and then falling into the water, accompanied by great shrieks of laughter from the crowds. There was a story told about him that during the War he rowed his barrel across the Channel to Dunkirk to help bring the British soldiers home. It can't have been true, but I like to think it was, and certainly the Hastings fishing fleet turned out for that rescue. In front of the unique black Tudor rope houses which had been used for storing nets for centuries, there was a barrow set up to delight curious day-trippers, bearing a sign "Wonders of the Deep", displaying a rather gruesome selection of strange fish that the fishermen found in their nets and which couldn't be sold at the Fish Market. I can now only remember the fish that had a ciga-rette stuck in its mouth by one old salt.

Granddad was by now crippled with rheumatoid arthritis and in great pain, his fingers twisted and gnarled. Even so, he still drew and painted simple pictures of Sussex churches, which at Christmas were printed and turned into cards and calendars and sold to neighbours. We loved to comb Grand-dad's silver hair and moustache with his big metal comb and beg him to tell us stories about when he was young, or about his life in the Army in India. He would bring out his memen-tos, little brightly painted clay figures of people dressed in exotic clothes, the Benares-ware cobras and a large (and dead) bronze-and-green monsoon beetle. We pushed him to cricket matches in his wheelchair, or out into the country, where the biggest mushrooms and the most luscious black-berries that we picked were always given to him.

Gran made a fierce cocoa of hot water without milk, and on the rare occasions when she made a jelly for tea, we always had to eat it with a slice of bread, which detracted somewhat from the treat. It was called "making things go round," and whenever we had dinner with Gran and asked what was for afters, it was always "Wait and see pudding."

In Granny's scullery hung her "bluebag", which she either added to her wash, or dabbed on you to relieve a wasp sting. I thought it was magic. And in her kitchen was a glass jar full of black-and-white striped humbugs and you were always allowed one if you'd fallen over and grazed your knees, with the admonition, "Make it last." In my autograph book—such a craze when we were schoolchildren—she wrote: "Be good, sweet maid, and let who will, be clever"—not only impossible advice, but giving out entirely the wrong message.

After Dad was demobbed and home again, he got a job as a laundry delivery man. This was fun for Dolly and me, as sometimes he'd take us on his round out into the country. We always got a meat pasty at the baker's at Sedlescombe, a great treat, and we felt so grand sitting in the front of the van occasionally being saluted by a patrolling uniformed AA man on motor bike and side-car. I loved seeing my Dad's tanned arms on the steering wheel, and we'd squeal as we bounced up in the air when he drove fast over hump-backed bridges, or when he turned the engine off and we coasted down hills. He was a sociable man and popular with his customers, and was frequently given the odd rabbit or eggs or piles of comics and *Girl's Crystal* magazines which kept us thankfully quiet for hours.

15

Alabama

To God and to the Lamb I will sing, I will sing
To God and to the Lamb I will sing
To God and to the Lamb, who is the great I Am
While millions join the theme, I will sing

WE WERE NOW DEEP IN THE HEART OF ALABAMA IN THE small town of Fyffe, where we spent the day recording Sacred Harp Singers at what was called "A Big Sing". Sometimes known as "Shape-note", Sacred Harp is one of the most extraordinary and thrilling sounds of the South. It had its beginnings in New England, and was part of the Protestant belief that church services shouldn't be conducted in Latin, but in English, and that the congregation could take part by singing hymns in their own tongue. With many settlers still unable to read *words*, let alone music, a form of sol-fa was devised in the late 18th-century by one Andrew Law, a singing school teacher. Called "Shape-note" notation, and based on four shapes, a circle, a square, a diamond and a triangle, it was reckoned to be easy to learn, and swept the country like wildfire throughout the 19th century. It was—and still is—one of the most vigorous forms of music to emerge from America. The words of many of the hymns were set to folk tunes—after all, wasn't it Charles Wesley who asked, "Why should the Devil have all the best tunes?"—tunes that were familiar to people in the rural South. This must have contributed to the enormous appeal of this form of church music.

The passion and vigour with which the people at Fyffe sang was astounding in its power and intensity. The singers stood on four sides around a leader, with basses on the left, trebles on the right, a mixed group of tenors and sopranos in front, and altos behind. It was a democratic system, where each member led a hymn in turn. The leader called out the number of his or her chosen song, and there was a buzz of anticipation as the singers riffled through the beautiful oblong Sacred Harp hymn book to the right page. The key note was set by the leader and repeated by the group. The leader intoned one line, the choir sang one verse through in sol-fa, then launched energetically into the words at a rattling pace. They sang at the tops of their natural voices, which were rough, harsh, strident and shrill, but the majesty and beauty of the sound was undeniable. It was thrilling and enthralling.

People had come from all over the South for this "Big Sing", and the ladies were dressed in their finery; there were many frilled blouses, feathered hats, glittering brooches and earrings, and rouged cheeks. They had pulled out all the stops for the midday picnic, since the gathering was as much a social as a religious event. Trestles had been set outdoors to

Howe Road Church. Rev Donalson

This is my ticket to New York.

Baptism service at 7 pm. on Wakeside street in Huntsville. Pastor man (f60) very intelligent & cordial, said its a great oppty to send voices to NY, I havent got a ticket, but this way I'm glad to go. Lots of children in congregatn. Pastor goes outside. Enters a man, white handkerchief on his head. He is blind. Singing. Then congregatn stand up sing. 14 to be baptised. Very beautiful singing. Then they join in singing along. I think those all dressed in white are sisters of the church, and day is the baptism. gul — on robe — 15. Blind man prays. While congregatn stands The baptism font is built rather behind the altar. Big wooden trap door opens from floor. This is the pool. Revs flat white flat baha style hat — white drill cotton robe, showing his khakis underneath. Flips his foot over on side white he preaches. "Strangely dressed,

The page from my notebook detailing the events at the gospel competition and baptism in Huntsville, Alabama.

form a table fifty feet long, and it was laden with dishes of cold chicken, pork and ham, sweet potato pies, country sausages, home-made beans, grape jelly, lemon meringue pies, chocolate cakes, pound cakes, angel-food cake—oh, almost everything you could name. I felt like Mole in *The Wind in the Willows* listening to Rat gallop through his picnic list.... "'Oh stop, stop,' cried the Mole in ecstasies: 'This is too much!'"

It was a memorable and wonderful day, the people were so hospitable, and "kindly pleased" to see a girl from England there, especially one who so obviously loved their music. One woman laughingly said, "After you've heard it awhile it's like whooping cough—it grows on you." One of the older ladies expressed surprise that I spoke their language so well, evidence, not of ignorance, but of the isolation of their lives. But there came an unpleasant reminder of white Southern attitudes when I told a farmer that we would be recording black church music next. It was the flat and unemotional way in which he spoke that distressed and frightened me. "We don't like niggers here and won't allow 'em. Nigger come up here last year and the boys run him to death with their guns. No sir, don't want no niggers here."

I shouldn't have been surprised, as in Alabama, Georgia and Mississippi, there were "KKK" signs up outside some towns, announcing the Klan's legal presence there. It pointed up the paradoxes of the South: Cruel and kind, mean and hospitable, illiterate and witty.

In the next couple of days we recorded a gospel competition and a baptism at a black church in a little side street in Huntsville. We'd been given permission by the pastor, a most intelligent and cordial man in his forties. "It's a great opportunity to send our voices to New York," he said. "I haven't got a ticket, but this way I'm glad to go." He was baptising his fifteen-year-old daughter. He had twelve children of his own, and they were all in church, the littlest curled up asleep, the older girls playing with each other's hair, giggling and whispering. An elderly blind man, with a white handkerchief tied over his head, walked singing down through the congregation, and as he passed, they stood and joined in the spiritual. Leading in the girl who was to be baptised came a group of smiling deacons, men and women, dressed in white cotton robes. On their heads the men wore white chefs' hats with the crowns flattened down, while the women wore waitresses' caps or head bands. The blind man began to pray. The pastor, also wearing white, entered from a side door. Two deacons pulled at a large iron ring on a trap door set in the floor to reveal the baptism pool.

"John the Baptist," said the pastor, "came out of the Wilderness. I don't know if he was able to sing or not, but he *was* able to *preach*, down by the banks of the river. Today they might misfortune him as a lunatic. Jesus himself wasn't well-equipped to do his job until he'd gone down to the river to be baptised by John!"

"Ha-ha!" roared the blind man, and slapped his hand against his knee.

The girl waiting to be baptised wore a towelling dressing-gown, and sat between two women. One of them put a bathing cap on her head, the other tied a cord around her ankles and helped her hobble to the steps of the pool. By now, the Pastor and two deacons were standing knee-deep in the water, and they helped her down. She jumped up and down, half-laughing, half-crying, shouting and screaming "Thank you Jesus!" over and over again. Her father clapped a cloth over her face and lowered her down on her back completely under the water. She came out *really* shouting. The congregation was weeping, laughing and clapping, and as the girl was dried and led away from the pool, they started to sing. The Pastor shook hands with the elders, the big trapdoor was lowered down over the pool, and as the carpet was rolled back over it, a few beetles crawled away, and the service continued.

Father and daughter re-emerged, he in a sharp brown suit, she in a purple silk dress, calm now. "If singing is the life of religion," said the Pastor, "Some people don't have any! They go to church and sit there with their mouths shut from the time they get there to the time they leave. Let's sing this together! Get ready! Leave this choir—join the Heavenly one and sing through ceaseless ages!" He took hold of his daughter's hand and sang "If I Never Get to See You Anymore". "I love to sing that song," he said. "It consoles me when nothing else won't. Take Christ for your weapon. He will fight your battles! We should rejoice to see one come out of the darkness into this marvellous light. She have repented—she have walked away from sin!"

The blind man hooted with joy.

The lady I was sitting next to, who had been alternately laughing and crying throughout the ceremony, turned to me and said, "I go to church to get happy. We *really* put it on when there's a corpse!"

> Dear Mum and Dolly,
>
> I hope everyone understands why it's so hard for me to write. You see, we travel and record all day. Take Sunday—we record from 9 till 1 o'clock at a Sacred Harp singing, then drive to Huntsville 65 miles away,

record a gospel competition till 6, then record a Negro baptism from 7.30 till 10, then drive off again and sleep in a motel...... And on our drive from Fyffe to Huntsville a front tyre burst and we went skidding along the road. And there was the Tennessee River running alongside the narrow road, and about a hundred yards ahead was a very high bridge which we might have been going across! Alan managed the car very well, though, but it was scary!

Shirley

16

Hastings 1950—Bobby Sox

WHEN DAD LEFT, UNCLE FRED, MUM'S BROTHER, VIRTUALLY took the place of our father. He was passionate about music and literature and would talk tirelessly about both, and we hung onto every word. His favourite composer was Henry Purcell. "Christ! Just listen to that!" he'd exclaim, eyes alight. He also loved the boogie-woogie of Jimmy Yancey. The latter was somewhat disapproved of by Mum who didn't like us listening to American pop music as she thought it was a corrupting influence, so I had to listen to my favourite singers like Guy Mitchell, Jo Stafford, Frankie Laine and Johnny Ray on the radio while Mum was out at work.

I longed to be able to jitterbug and I loved the fashions of the dancers that we saw in American films, especially the full skirts and anklesocks of the girls who were being thrown over their partners' shoulders. You may chortle at this, but I recall many years later when I was on tour with The Albion

Me, Mum and Dolly on the iron bridge, Coghurst.

Dance Band in Brittany in the 1970s, our French organiser, a very pretty young woman, wore white anklesocks with high heeled shoes, and all the men in the band were beside themselves with lust agreeing it was the height of sexy chic!

17

Mississippi

It ain't but the one thing I done wrong
Stayed in Mississippi just a day too long

SOME OF THE MOST REMARKABLE RECORDINGS THAT ALAN AND his father John Lomax made were in the 1930s and '40s in the Mississippi State Penitentiary, Parchman Farm. There they found the majestic worksongs, blues and field hollers of the black convicts. I had known the music for some time and thought it one of the noblest sounds I had ever heard. There was a special quality to those early recordings made out in the fields, the songs punctuated by the fall of the prisoners' hammers or hoes, with an occasional piece of wood or chunk of stone hitting the microphone. The songs and the voices were superb, and I often felt guilty at finding it so thrilling since I knew that the men were incarcerated, and often for no other reason than that they were black. There were many

F. W. THORNHILL
COMMISSIONER

J. P. COLEMAN, GOVERNOR
W. M. BLACK
CHAIRMAN, BOARD OF COMMISSIONERS

M. E. THOMPSON
COMMISSIONER

Mississippi State Penitentiary.

BILL HARPOLE
SUPERINTENDENT

E. E. LACEY
ASSISTANT SUPERINTENDENT

J. D. SISTRUNK, SR.
AGRONOMIST

K. K. STINSON, D. V. M.
DIRECTOR OF LIVESTOCK
PRODUCTION

F. H. LINSKEY
SECRETARY

E. B. HEARN
CLASSIFICATION OFFICER

R. L. PATTERSON, JR.
EDUCATIONAL DIRECTOR

R. B. HICKS
CHAPLAIN

PARCHMAN. MISSISSIPPI

Dearest Mum, Dolly and Jonathan,

Well, they finally got us at last ! Alan is out working with
the convicts, I'm sitting in the superintendant's house being
interviewed by the State Parole Board.
I'd expected the Pen to be a big, grim grey fortress.
Instead it's a 23,000 acre plantation, where they grow enormous
amounts of cotton, corn, vegetables, fruit, peants. 2,000 convicts,
white and Negro, thirty only women. They work in the fields all
day, or can food, and sew.Sleep in large barrack buildings, with
hospital-type beds, curtains at the windows as well as bars. They
are free all day, locked up at night. The compounds are planted
with grass and flowers, they are allowed pets. ery well fed and
well looked after physically. The work songs aren't as primitive
and despairing as they were when conditions were bad. It's smoother,
rounder, calmer, sweeter, less exciting. Today Alan has found a man
that sings like a turtle dove, he says, but I haven't heard him
since I'm not allowed out with Alan in the fields or the camps.

This stereophonic recording is fantastically beautiful to listen
to, but exhausting to make. Four mikes, miles upon miles of wires,
all sorts of gadgets around that people walk over and fall over.
I told you about the Scared Harp, didn't I, in Fyfe, Alabama, where
the poeple really were hospitable, cooperative, pleased for us to
record " so that all the world can hear the old hymns." But back in
Kentucky, where we recorded Old Regular Baptist hymns, we were met
with suspicion, hostility and in many cases, refusal. We had
permission from the local minister at Blackie, Kentucky, to record
the convention at the hill, an open stand on the mountain side,
a natural pulpit you might say, five miles back from the main road.
A dirt track just wide enough to let a car through. Here the preachers
from all over Kentucky gathered, to preach and lead the singing.
He lines out the one line at a time, the same tune, then after each
line the congrehation sings the real tune, swelling it out, and
the sound soars across the hills and echoes round the valleys. It
stops your heart when you first hear it. So, we dragged the
machinery up there; put it up with great difficulty - no electricity
of course, so we used two heavy batteries. We worked for about an hour
getting the positions right, and the right balance . THEN - one old
preacher stood up when it was his turn to preach, and said, "I've been
preaching all my life without the aid of them phones. No ane asked me
if they could be here, and I don't know who's responsible, but I
ain't gonna say one single word until them things is gone." There
was nothing to do but take them down. He was a real old timer,
a strict, Primitive Hard-Shell Baptist. Said my bobbed hair was
sinful and an abomination ytO the Lord. The machine was an invention

My original letter home, written on Parchman Farm notepaper.

stories along these lines: when a black man was picked up by white cops, he protested, "I ain't done nothing!"

'Well, we gonna arrest you in *advance*—you bound to do somethin'!"

Alan had long wanted to return, and here we were on our way to Parchman, permission having been given by the Mississippi prison board. I was at once excited and scared; we had to be on our guard, and it wasn't the convicts we had most to fear. The further South we went, the more apprehensive I became, knowing that the Deep South was the home of the Ku Klux Klan.

To an onlooker it might have appeared as if we were driving into Parchman waving a white flag of surrender. We'd been on the road for nearly a month and we and our clothes were getting travel worn. In order to have a reasonable appearance and make a good impression when we met the prison Superintendent, I had washed Alan's best white shirt that morning at our motel. It was still damp and I was hanging it out of the car window trying to dry it in the breeze. It was a somewhat futile effort because in that heat we were bathed in sweat most of the time, anyway, but it gave me something to concentrate on as we headed towards the Penitentiary across the Delta country that was flat and wide as far as the eye could see. I felt a very long way from home.

I knew that Parchman was a prison farm, but I had imagined it as a huge grey fortress. Instead it was a vast open plantation of 20,000 acres, producing cotton, corn, sugar, vegetables and fruit. Its huge profits were made from the labour of the convicts, 2,000 of them, mostly black, who worked from "cain't to cain't"—from when you can't see in the morning until you can't see at night; sun-up to sun-down. It

Alan's photos
taken at Parchman Farm,
Mississippi State
Penitentiary.

didn't seem to me to be much different from a slave plantation. The men worked in the fields or in the canning factory or the dairy watched by armed guards, and slept at night in large barracks with barred windows. To be fair to the authorities, the food given the prisoners looked good and plentiful.

I wasn't allowed out in the fields when Alan was recording but had to stay inside, and coped instead with the Mississippi Parole Board who were visiting at the same time. I was asked a few questions about my background, surprise expressed that I was such a long way from home and travelling alone with an older man. I explained that I had worked for Alan in England, and that this was a wonderful opportunity and experience for me. Alan had warned me not to show any anger at segregation while we were there as it could be dangerous, and would certainly jeopardise our work. One member of the board, an unpleasant red-neck with an over-familiar manner asked me what I thought of "niggers".

"Oh," I replied, keeping my face expressionless so as not to show my loathing of him, "We don't have any where I come from in England." I was able to say it absolutely truthfully, because it was actually true.

"How fortunate you are," he replied. Later he cornered me and tried to kiss me. When I pushed him away and threatened to find the Superintendent's wife, he said, "Well, young lady, don't put any more weight on, or *nobody*'ll want to kiss you." The gratuitous insult sickened me, and I felt desperately sorry for the poor prisoners whose futures were in the hands of such a man.

The Superintendent and his wife, the Harpoles, were courteous and hospitable to us both, and didn't hinder Alan in his work, although they may not have understood his interest. I found it frustrating to be housebound, but I tried to befriend the black woman who cleaned my room, one of only thirty female prisoners. She was nervous of talking to me and wouldn't look me in the face—I suppose she thought I would report back—but on the day before we left, she trusted me enough to tell me that she had been arrested for walking down a railroad track. She was illiterate and hadn't been able to read the "No Trespassing" sign.

We were in Parchman for three days. Alan found that the music, in the intervening seventeen years since he'd first recorded there, had lost something of its grandeur and despair. It may have been that conditions, although still harsh, were not as brutal as they had been, or perhaps it was that the younger prisoners didn't want to keep up the old way of singing and the old songs. It frustrates me that because my stay at Parchman was both brief and constrained, I can't properly convey what life was like there, but Alan has written about it in his book *The Land Where The Blues Began* (Pantheon, NY 1992), rightly called his tour-de-force, winning the American National Book Critics' Award for non-fiction in 1993.

The quality of the music, and of Alan's recordings of it, remain undiminished to this day, so much so, that some forty years on, those remarkable film-makers Ethan and Joel Coen used a track from the 1959 Parchman Farm recordings in their film *O Brother, Where Art Thou*. The song was a worksong, "Po' Lazarus", and the lead singer, one James Carter. The soundtrack was voted best album of the year at the Grammy Awards in 2002, and the CD sold over five million copies. Alan's daughter, Anna Lomax Wood and Don Fleming, director of licensing for the Lomax Estate, traced

James Carter, seventy-six years old at the time, to Chicago. They presented him with a royalty cheque for $20,000, the first of many, and flew him and his wife to the Grammy Awards in Los Angeles. There is occasionally some justice in this world.

When it was time to leave, the relief was enormous. Alan was exhausted by what had been a gruelling three days for him, physically, mentally and emotionally. When we'd driven some miles from Parchman, he asked me to take the wheel. I was still learning to drive the Buick, and as it was straightforward motoring on the endlessly long, straight and empty roads of the Delta, I took over. I'd only driven a few miles when we were flagged down by two highway patrolmen. My heart was in my mouth. I didn't have a driving licence, not even a provisional one, and worse, I didn't have a passport or a visa with me, as both were in an office in Nashville, waiting for an extension to my stay to be approved. I had visions of being taken straight back to prison. As I drew up, one of them raised his hat, leaned through the window and said very politely, "Ma'am, there's been an accident up ahead, the road's closed. Just make a U-turn here and take the detour further back at the sign."

I'd never done a U-turn before, but I managed to execute it perfectly and drove calmly away—the calm of complete shock! When I was out of sight of the patrolmen, I started to shake, my knees gave out, and I didn't dare drive for a long while after that.

We were heading out of the fertile Delta into the more hilly and wooded country of Northern Mississippi, where Alan was hoping to find Sid Hemphill, a black fiddle player he'd recorded back in the '40s. We stopped for a night's rest in

Sid Hemphill and Lucius Smith.

Oxford, William Faulkner's home town, where a friendly bar-
tender in the hotel gave us the name of a local relief admin-
istrator who he thought might be able to help. Sure enough,
his patch was Panola County, he knew of Sid, and drove with
us to Senatobia. It was very dry here, the soil so eroded that
there were great cracks in the earth as wide as the car's
wheel. The land might be parched, but it was going to yield
us the richest harvest of the trip.

Sid, ninety-one years old, remembered Alan and greeted
him warmly. He still played fiddle and what he called "the
quills". These were panpipes which he blew across, leaning
his head over them. Then he'd tip his head back to whoop
and hoot between the phrases of the tune, making music
that sounded primitive and African to my ears. He was blind
and carried a walking stick with a carved alligator climbing up one side and over the top. Around his neck he wore
a dried corn cob on a string "to keep the rheumatiz away",

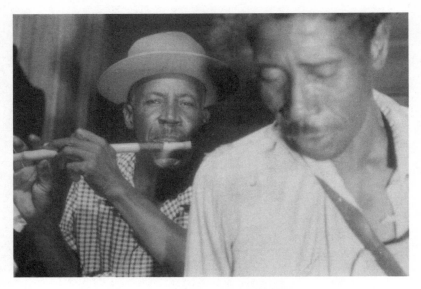

Ed and Lonnie Young, Como, Mississippi.

while his little granddaughter had a nickel on a string round hers to help with teething. Did she just bite on it, or was it supposed to have some magical properties? I didn't like to ask, but learned later it was a voodoo charm.

Sid was soon joined by his old friend Lucius Smith on banjo and drums, and they played with a zest and energy that belied their age. It was wonderfully attractive, this combination of African sounds and Southern dance tunes. It was music they had known since boyhood, and had played for years at country picnics, tunes with evocative names like "Natchez Under the Hill", "Billy in the Lowground", "Hell Among the Yearlings". Sid's daughter, Mrs Sidney Carter, was a fine blues singer and guitarist, and we recorded through the evening. One of her songs, "Didn't Leave Nobody But the Baby" was also to appear on the *O Brother Where Art Thou* soundtrack, although not her original recording.

As we left that night, Sid told us of other black musicians nearby in Como that he thought we'd like to hear.

So, next day, we drove further into this eroded landscape to Como, where the brothers Lonnie and Ed Young lived. We inched slowly over the ruts and into a clearing where hens scratched, mangy dogs came barking round the car and the children playing there ran to hide behind their mothers' skirts. Lonnie came out of one of the tumble-down wooden shacks and greeted us cautiously. I often wondered what apprehension people felt at the approach of a big car with two white strangers in it. But Alan's reassuring magic quickly went to work, there was a warm response to his friendliness, enthusiasm and gentle manners, his warm chuckle, and soon the music was underway.

Lonnie played with his brother, Ed, and their music was even more primitive than Sid's had been the night before. Lonnie played a cane whistle which he called a "fiste". He started a song or tune with several weaving lines of melody, then Ed came in drumming slowly and insistently, driving the tune along. Several women joined in with hand-clapping and formed a circle round Ed. Still drumming, he started to dance.

He was a compelling sight, with a shock of hair that stood upright and added several inches to his height. As he danced, he slowly turned and wound himself down into the ground, like a serpent coiling. I was completely spellbound watching this man reduce himself in size, the women rhythmically clapping him on. When he was level with the earth, the women bent down and drummed the ground with their hands. He swept his hand over the dust then brushed it across his forehead, leaving a white mark. As he slowly uncoiled and regained his full height, I turned to look at Alan to convey my wonder at what I'd seen. Like me, he had tears in his eyes. We were both overwhelmed by witnessing this ancient ritual, the feeling heightened by the remoteness of the place we were in. Later Alan said that it was like watching Pan dance, and there was magic there for sure.

There were tears one minute, laughter the next. After we'd recorded a song with the lines:

Jim and John had a race

Jim beat John to the best old place

I asked Lonnie where "the best old place" was. I had a dim recollection of songs about riverboat races on the Mississippi, and thought it was one of those. Then, as he grinned, I realised too late its sexual connotation. I burst out laughing and the laughter spread through the group, women burying their heads in their aprons wiping tears away. In the next song, there was another couplet...

Hen duck said to the drake

No more cat-fish in the lake

.....but I'd got the drift by then and kept quiet. There was a wonderful atmosphere and feeling that had grown up between us all, one of friendship and trust. We recorded well into the night, and arranged to continue the next day.

In the morning, the children asked if they could record some singing-games, and with much giggling and clapping they did so.

"I'm a little acorn nut,

I lay on the cuckoo ground

Peoples come and step on me,

That is why I'm cracked you see

Opposite page: Lonnie Young (top left) and Ed Young (top right and below).

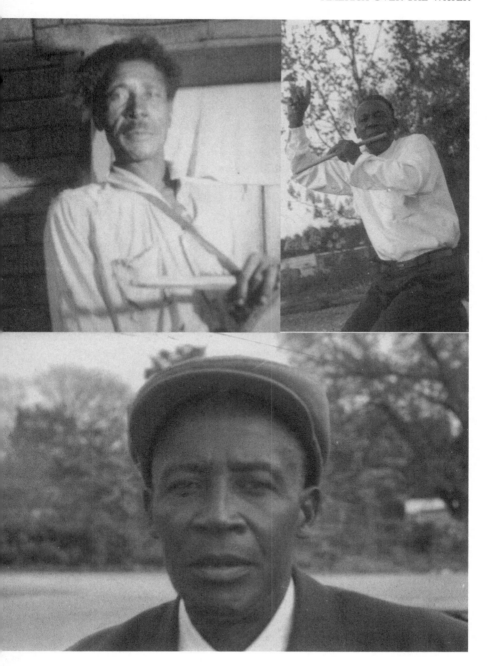

I'm a nut, I'm a nut—I'm crazy!
Talk to myself on the telephone
Just to hear my golden tone
Ask myself for a date—
Meet you here at half past eight.
Take myself to the picture show
Just because I love me so
Put my arms around my waist—
If I get fresh I slap my face
I can sing, I can dance,
I wear ruffles on my—OOPS, Boys,
Take another guess,
I wear ruffles on my dress!"

We were joined that afternoon by the elderly Pratcher brothers, Miles and Bob, who played old tunes on fiddle and guitar. They too had that same quality that, for me, defined the black music of that part of Northern Mississippi, a buoyant drive, no matter what the age of the musician. Again, I had no need to enquire what their song "All Night Long" was about.

Lonnie said he'd asked another neighbour to come by in the evening, a younger man who played blues. Towards dusk, a slight figure in dungarees and carrying a guitar appeared out of the trees and walked into the clearing. Lonnie introduced him. His name was Fred McDowell, he was a fifty year old farmer and he'd been picking cotton all day. I am ashamed to say that at first I resented the intrusion by a younger man into the atmosphere made by the old musicians with their ancient and fascinating sounds. I didn't want that spell broken. Fred started to play bottleneck guitar, a shim-

Annie Mae and Mississippi Fred McDowell.

mering and metallic sound. His singing was quiet but strong and with a heart-stopping intensity. By the time he'd finished his first blues, we knew we were in the presence of a great and extraordinary musician. He sang "61 Highway".

Lord, the 61 Highway,
Is the only road I know
She runs from New York City,
Right down by my baby's door
Now some folks say the Greyhound buses don't run
Just go to West Memphis, baby,
Look down Highway 61

I said please, please see somebody for me
If you see my baby,
Tell her she's alright with me
Lord if I should ever die, baby,
Before you think my time have come
I want you to bury my body down on Highway 61.

Alan wrote one word in his notebook. "Perfect".

We could only record Fred at night, as he was getting his cotton crop in during the day. We were there for four nights. One night a storm blew up, a majestic thunderstorm that was unlike anything I'd ever experienced. It seemed like there were six storms raging at once. The sky was as bright as day with continuous blue lightning, fantastic sheet lightning that quite literally lit up all the countryside around, and forked lightning that flashed along the massive cloud formations before it struck down into the earth so powerfully that the ground trembled. The thunder roared and cracked, accompanied by a strange and eerie wind that had sprung up.

Everyone said the storm was some distance off and wasn't coming our way, so we all stood outside and watched it for a while—Lonnie's little two room wooden shack didn't offer much protection anyway. Within half an hour, one part of the storm came directly overhead, and a particularly violent flash shook the house, taking out all the electricity. There was no point attempting to set up the batteries because the rain hammering the tin roof sounded like we were under Niagara Falls. We gave up at 3 a.m.

We continued the next night recording blues and spirituals from Fred, some with his wife Annie Mae, some with his

Opposite: Mississippi Fred McDowell, photographed by Alan.

FRED & ANNIE MAE McDOWELL   "MY HOME IS IN THE DELTA"   TESTAMENT T-2208
Waiting for my baby/I'm in jail again/The girl I'm loving/Going down South, carry my
whip/Diving duck blues/The sun rose this morning/Get right church*/Amazing Grace*/
Jesus gonna make up my dying bed*/Where could I go*/The Lord will make a way*/Keep
your lamp trimmed and burning*/When the Saints*
Fred McDowell (vcl.gtr) with Annie Mae McDowell (vcl on *)
    Fred McDowell, discovered a few years ago by Alan Lomax and Shirley Collins in Como
Miss. has proved to be perhaps the most important traditional 'discovery' of all. His
first LP on Arhoolie was magnificent; so is Pete Welding's album, which for one side
follows the pattern of its predecessor. McDowell's solid guitar playing and splendid
bottleneck are well showcased on the first six tracks. As usual, what goes in is for
the most part traditional song, and what comes out is all McDowell. "Girl I'm lovin"
and "Divin' duck" for example are derived from Sleepy John Estes originals, but Fred
gives them new scope and no hint of derivitiveness. The accompaniment to the former is
masterly, bottleneck echoing every slightest emotion in the singing. "The sun rose"
has a superb lyric and shows the scope of McDowell's ability as a storyteller. But on
the flipside Welding's amazing daring comes in; and comes off beautifully. Perhaps the
one track with wife Annie on Arhoolie formed a precedent but the side of religious numbers was an inspiration. One baulks at comparing anyone with Willie Johnson and his
wife but this couple come as good as I've ever heard. This is exciting, moving, honest
-to-goodness country spiritual the like of which should have vanished from record many
years ago. Again we are indebted to Pete Welding and his great label for some of the
best of its kind in catalogue. This is a fine, interesting valuable record with most
interesting notes, cover photo and thoroughly recommended to all.   Simon A. Napier
----
SOUNDS & FURY: A new magazine for Jazz and Blues has begun publication. Edited by
Charles Fero "Sounds and Fury" has little blues as yet, but more is promised. Glossy
and very proffessional, it must interest anyone with tastes for traditional or modern
jazz. A special reduced rate subscription offer is available now at 7 dollars (50/-)
the first 10 issues. Write "S&F" 1121 Bleecker St., Utica, N.Y.. Good luck.....

September 1965   Page 24   Blues Unlimited 25

Review of Fred McDowell's first album in *Blues Unlimited* magazine,
autographed by Fred.

sister Fanny Davis who played comb and paper, a combination that may sound risible, but was in fact touchingly sweet
and tender. By the time we had to leave to go on to Arkansas,
we had grown very close. I felt such admiration for Fred and
such affection for his wife Annie Mae, that as we were saying
goodbye, I kissed her on the cheek. A silence fell over the
gathering, and I thought I had done something wrong, but
Alan told me later it was probably the first time people there
had seen a white woman kiss a black one.

I was so fortunate, so privileged to have been there at the
discovery—for the outside world—of Mississippi Fred McDow-

Name	Address	Phone No.	Birth-days	Anniver-saries	Christmas	Valentine's Day	Easter	Other Occasions
Mr & Mrs Harpole, Parchman, Miss.								
Viola James, Rte 2, Box 92,	Como, Miss							
Lonnie Young – Rte 1, Como –								
Ed Young – 1463 Dunn St, Apt 30, Memphis								
Fred McDowell – Rte 1, Como.								
Miles & Bob Pratcher, Rte 1, Como.								
James Shorty – Rte 2, Box 11, Senatobia.								
Almeda Riddle – Rte 3, Box 122, Heber Springs,								Ark.
Neal Morris – Mountainview, Ark								
Jimmy Driftwood, Timbo, Ark.								
Ollie & Oscar Gilbert, Timbo, Ark.								

Page from my original address book kept during the trip.

ell, who justly became world-famous once people had heard these first recordings. He went on to make several more albums, and gave many concerts in America and Europe. He was taken up by the Rolling Stones, and it is said that he was buried in the silver lamé suit they bought him. My delight at his success is tempered by the fact that he died thirteen years after our meeting, and I wonder if the new lifestyle that we inadvertently led him to hastened his death. All I can say is that Fred was overjoyed to be able to make his recordings for us. As Alan said, "He knew he had been heard and felt his fortune had been made."

For my part, I shall never forget the first sight I had of Fred in his dungarees, carrying his guitar and walking out of the trees towards us in a Mississippi night.

18

Hastings 1950—The Flicks

BACK THEN, BEFORE TV BECAME COMMONPLACE IN THE home, the radio was all important—indeed crucial to my career as it turned out. My favourite programmes both featured folk music; *Country Magazine* which had a listening audience each week of an amazing 12-15 million people, and *As I Roved Out*, field recordings from the British Isles. Some of the songs I knew already, and even those I hadn't heard before seemed familiar to me, and I loved the tunes. I was absolutely captivated by this music, and by the age of fifteen I knew that I wanted to be a folk singer. Dolly bought a cheap Czechoslovakian guitar on instalments through an advertisement in *The Daily Worker* (Mum by then having become an ardent socialist as well as an early feminist), and we sang for hours at the top of our stairs where there was a perfect echo.

In any case, I had already been influenced by a Hollywood film called *Night Club Girl*. Mum used to give Dolly and me ten shillings every Saturday, and for that ten bob we could go "down town" on the bus, go to the pictures and get lunch for two. We'd have lunch (but then we called it dinner) at Lyons in Hastings, where we always had baked beans and chips served in small oblong dishes which you helped yourself to from behind the glass doors of the hatches at the self service counter. The food was always dried out and crusty at the edges. Delicious. We loved it. Then for afters we'd have a trifle served in the same shaped dish, and then off to the flicks.

There were five cinemas in Hastings and St Leonards; the Gaiety opposite the cricket ground; the Ritz boasting a "mighty Wurlitzer organ" which rose out of the floor as the screen showed all the words of the songs with a little ball bouncing along them so you could sing along; the Regal, rather optimistically named; the Curzon, where even into the late 1970s you could order tea and biscuits to be brought to your seat during the interval; and heading towards the Old Town, the fishing end, was the DeLuxe, known locally as "the flea-pit".

In those days, two films were shown, for each programme, an A- and a B-movie. *Night Club Girl*, a B-movie, was the story of a Kentucky backwoods girl who went to the city and sang her folk songs in a night club. Naturally, the club owner fell in love with her, and as he was played by an actor I was crazy about, I thought, "That'll do for me. I'm going to be a folk singer. I'll write to the BBC and let them know!"

The Gods were smiling—the letter was passed to Bob Copper of the Copper family of Rottingdean in Sussex, whose own tradition of folk song went back through many generations. He was one of the BBC's official folk music collectors, and while he and his colleague John Sharp were in Hastings recording songs from the fishermen in the Old Town, they followed up my letter and visited us. It's a chance I almost ruined, as for some reason, instead of singing some of the songs Great Granny and the family sang, I tried to impress with a Scottish ballad which I'd learned from the radio, and which I daresay I tried to sing with a Scots accent!

It was only due to Bob's understanding and his ever-present sense of humour that he encouraged us to continue with our music, instead of belittling us as he could have done. He also noticed how hard-up we were, and he paid Mum a fee for her singing of some country dance tunes and steps. I'm sure this came out of his own pocket, and I never forgot this act of kindness. I was to renew the acquaintance a few years later. Bob was passionate about the Blues, and he and Alan formed a friendship while both were working for the BBC in the 1950s. It was wonderful to meet him again, and thereafter become firm friends up until his death in 2004. This lovely Sussex man was uniquely gifted as a writer, historian, raconteur and singer, and he lit and warmed my life as he did countless others.

19

Arkansas

Shoot your dice and have your fun, Sugar Babe
Shoot your dice and have your fun
Run like the devil when the po-lice come....

O N THE AFTERNOON OF OCTOBER 1ST 1959, WE DROVE INTO the town of Hughes, Arkansas, where Alan was looking for a white saloon bar owner that blues men Big Bill Broonzy, Memphis Slim and Sonny Boy Williamson had told him about, a white man who was the best friend they had in the South. His name was Charlie Houlin, and it was said that to protect one of his black workers, he'd shot a white sheriff through the heart. That was in Hughes, and here we were, outside a saloon with a sign over the door, "Houlin's Place". Alan left me in the car and went inside, where sure enough, he found Charlie Houlin. Alan explained his mission, that he was looking for black musicians. Charlie told him he should go and find Forrest City Joe at another place, a gambling den called "The Old Whiskey Store". Alan decided that this was possibly a place it would be better for him to visit without me, so he took me back to Memphis, Tennessee, and booked me into a hotel. He then drove away across the state border back into Arkansas in search of the blues.

That first afternoon and all that night he recorded Forrest City Joe Pugh with his band, Boy Blue with His Two, energetic, rough, tough, erotic music, sounds that were later to be sampled by Moby. Charlie Houlin came by to listen in the early hours of the morning, and suggested to Alan that he head off next day to West Memphis, where he'd hear equally good blues, but suggested that he clear it with the local sheriff first, for, as he said, "They keep West Memphis pretty tied down."

West Memphis, Arkansas, was a gangster-ridden town with a corrupt police force, and within a couple of hours Alan was arrested for being in the black part of town, although he *had* spoken to the sheriff. He was picked up by two white cops as he sat in a gambling joint listening to the music. They asked him what he was doing there, searched him, searched the car, hauled him off to the police station, where he was questioned for an hour before the Sheriff's wife confirmed that Alan had checked with her husband first as Charlie had instructed. It made no difference. They refused to allow him to record any more music, but told him to get in the car and get the wheels rolling!

I was relieved when Alan showed up again—he'd been absent for two nights, and I was convinced something bad had happened to him. When he told me the story I was so relieved he was safe that I burst out laughing and said it

Forrest City Joe,
Hughes, Arkansas.

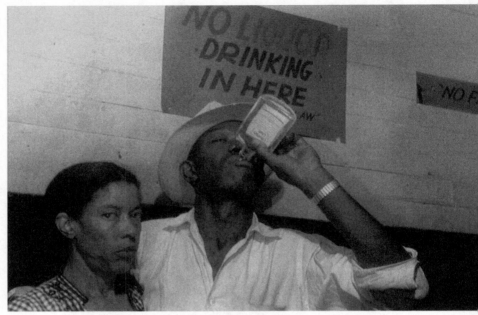

sounded like one huge cliché! Nevertheless, I knew the danger had been very real.

He played me his recordings, and even those sounded full of menace. Willie Jones of Boy Blue with His Two singing:

"You got dimples in your jaws, You's my baby, got my eyes on you...." and sounding like a rougher, coarser Muddy Waters, held such a powerful and dangerous sexual charge that my knees went weak.

Right in the centre of Memphis stood the Pentecostal Holiness Temple, a large, new, imposing building which we visited on October 4th. We met Bishop Patterson, a cool, dignified and very well-dressed black preacher. He drove a large new Cadillac which put our old Buick to shame, and he travelled around the country preaching, carrying his equipment in a large pantechnicon. In this temple we heard modern church music, with an orchestra of organ, drums, piano, clarinets and guitars, playing to a large and equally well-dressed congregation, clapping their hands and stamping their feet, rocking the church with the hymn "Power! *That's* the Power! *God's* the Power! *We* are the power!"

In a black Memphis suburb we found New Brown's Greater Harvest Church, and asked the minister, the Reverend Crenshaw, if his congregation still sang the old hymns. He said he thought some of the older members might remember them, and he allowed us to record an old lining hymn, to which he added a roaring sermon throughout, "I LOVE the Lord, he hears my cry... Long as I live where trouble ride..."

It put me in mind of the Kentucky mountainside gathering again. "Wild and terrifying," I wrote in my notebook.

He insisted that we also record their current spirituals accompanied on their brand new piano, a much faster rhythm with a syncopated jazz beat, "I'm goin' home on the morning train, yeah, yeah, yeah, yeah, yeah..."

Next day we drove away from the city, heading for the deep country, up into the Ozarks to visit Jimmy Driftwood, taking him up on the invitation he'd issued in July at the Berkeley Festival where we first met him. He wanted us to meet his father, Neal Morris, a fine singer of the old songs. Jimmy lived with his wife, Cleda, and two sons James and Bing, way back in Timbo: "Not a town, just a wide place in the road," was how Jimmy described it. His home was full of fiddles, banjos and mouthbows, most of them home-made, the finest of which he'd made from a bed-head, and the roughest from a fence post!

He'd written many songs, but also sang those he'd learned from his Dad, or "soaked up through my hide" as he put it. Neal also played guitar to accompany himself, and his sing-

Oscar Gilbert

ing voice was light, melodious and full of character. Between them they had a great number of songs of British origin. One of them was set in the Court of Queen Bess, and then, just in case I didn't know who that was, Neal reminded me she was Queen Elizabeth, otherwise known as Bonny Black Bess! He was full of stories about the little community of Timbo, the "hell-raising and rip-snorting" inhabitants, all the intrigues, scandals and killings. He told us of several "notrocious" local outlaws: "My father knew Frank and Jesse James—they crossed the county line and came to his house many time. And *he* knew there was many of them crimes laid to Frank and Jesse James, that he *knew* they didn't commit because they was at his house when they were *supposed* to be done! But you can't tell the public that! Once the public's made up its mind, why, it's a-gonna stick to it!"

Timbo, as I said, was way back in the hills, and the customs of the pioneers still prevailed. For instance, at the house of Oscar and Ollie Gilbert, who had sons and daughters and their families visiting, Alan was taken off into a room with the men, and I was banished to sit with the womenfolk. Men were served first at dinner—we ate when they'd finished. Oscar, 75 and blind for the last three years, was the local bully, "the fightingest man in the county." He was reputed to have killed seven men in his lifetime over two things—women and whiskey, and he was also the man who *made* the best moonshine. I tasted some—it was fiery! Surprisingly, he was a fine and gentle singer, and several of his tunes were of pure Irish origin.

So there I was with his wife Ollie, and we started talking. She was blind in one eye and said she'd lost it through being poisoned, but later one of her daughters confided to me that

Oscar had put it out in a fit of rage. In spite of all, she was sweet-natured, kind and friendly. She knew many songs which she sang in a gentle voice, some fine ballads with their roots in the British Isles, and she was fascinated to hear me sing versions of *her* songs that I knew from home. I felt an enormous sense of satisfaction and achievement in drawing her songs out in such an enjoyable way, recording a dozen or so.

After some four hours of talking and singing, I needed the lavatory, and asked her where it was. She took me down the garden to the outhouse, and there was the usual rough wooden hut, but with a difference. This one was a two-seater! I waited for her to go outside, but she hoicked up her skirt and apron, sat down on one and patted the edge of the other, waiting for me to use it. "Oh, when in Arkansas...." I thought, and sat down next to her. When we were settled side by side she poked me in the ribs with her elbow, grinned at me and said, "Shirley, now I'm going to sing you an *ugly* song!" "What's an ugly song, Ollie?" I asked. She nudged me again with her sharp elbow and replied, "Oh, you know, an *ugly song!*", and with her hands over her mouth, gave me a couple of extremely coarse songs. When we'd finished, we went back up the garden to the house, where she turned into a sweet old Granny again!

I thought back to when we'd been at Jimmy Driftwood's house a couple of days earlier and I'd needed the lav. I asked his wife Cleda where it was and was told to go outside. I looked right round the garden but I couldn't see the outhouse, so I asked again. "Oh hon', you just step outside and take your pick," she laughed. Jimmy, who must have made a not

Timbo, Arkansas
March 14, 1960

Dear Shirley: And tomorrow is the Ides of March to the World, but to
Uncle Zebob in Possum Holler, it's just The 2nd Tuesday in March, the moon
is full and it is a "durned" good time to plant "pertaters" if there
wasn't a foot of snow on the ground.

Uncle Absie Morrison spent the night with me not long ago and fiddled
while Cleda watched the tape machine and I made a Ham & Gravy dinner with
crackling cornbread. Uncle Absie spoke very kindly of that "purty girl
from England" and wondered when she would be traipsin on Cellar Creek
again.

Ollie Gilbert"has her hands full of a blind husband these days" and Oscar
says though he is blind, he still sees more than a lot of folks could see
if they had half a dozen eyes. Ollie always asks about you, and she really
liked you very much. Maybe when you come back you two can get together and
record an album of "Outhouse Ballads".

They say that Doctor Wolf is very "porely" and he can't be "holped". I'll
try to see him next week. I'm going to Nashville to entertain the
International Club at Peabody College, and then on the New York.

Shirley, I understand that I have a lot of fans in England. I would very
much like to come there for a while. I could have gone to India for several
weeks, but no, I'd much rather go to England. I'd like to do several kinds
of program there. British Ballads From The Ozarks should be interesting to
the people there. Of course I could do American Ballads on several subjects.
Driftwood at Sea might go well there, or Songs that came out of the Civil
War--Cowboy songs or American Indian in the British tongue.

How The West Was Won, 34 songs, in the album I did with Bing Crosby, Rosemary
Clooney, Sam Hinton and the Mormon Tabernacle Choir has been released as the
greatest collection of Western songs ever put together and I think it will
be a good album.

My own album, The Westward Movement, will be out April 1st, and I'd like to
send you a copy if you don't mind. The three films (Educational) I did,
have been released.

Shirley, I'm sending you some clippings, with extra copies of some and
extra pictures to send on to Jack Elliott. I like Jack very much and
want you to let him know as much. When and if I ever get to England I
want to see Jack, too.

Shirley, we were honored to have you with us, and look forward to the
time when you may come here and stay a long time. Cleda, James & Bing
join me in sending you all our affection in one big imaginary cake.

Lovingly
Jimmie Driftwood
Cleda, James & Bing.

Letter to me from Jimmy Driftwood, after my return to England.

inconsiderable amount in music royalties grinned and said
to Cleda, "You know, we ought to build a rest-room now!"

The area was fascinating, settled by English, Irish and
Scots, but it was also Indian country. The mouthbows that

Neal Morris

Jimmy played must surely have come from Indian culture, and were, indeed, made by a one-sixteenth Choctaw Indian, Jimmy's neighbour, 84 year-old Charlie Everidge, a retired forestry worker. White-haired and still handsome, Charlie lived alone at the edge of the forest with his two dogs, who obviously worshipped him. Neal Morris, his life-long friend took us to see him at seven o'clock one morning.

Charlie's wooden house, set back amongst trees at the end of a dusty track, was an entrancing sight. One half of the outside was painted a pinky-red and the other half pasted with red and pink pictures cut out from magazines. His porch top was decorated with car licence plates and hub caps that gleamed in the early morning sun. Inside the shack was just the one room, smoky and smelling of soot. There was an iron bedstead covered with a grimy patchwork quilt, two old rocking chairs, a bench and a table, and a wood stove with its iron chimney going straight out through a hole in the roof. He started or finished almost every sentence with the words "By Jude!", and his memory came and went. Sometimes he'd forgotten what had happened five minutes before, but he could remember what his Grandfather had told him of his early life.

"I lived with my grandfather at the head of Sycamore Creek," he said. "I was up there living in the forest. They used to make bows and all to shoot lizards and kill squirrels and things—or anything I wanted to shoot."

Alan wanted to know about the mouth-bow that he played. He laughed. "Took the bow up to my mouth one day, thumped it and it roared! Made a racket! Of course, there wasn't no guitars about then. Just made a cross string from a leather-wood bush. I was raised up creek, one family in three or four

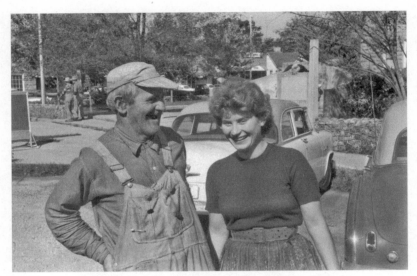

Charlie Everett and me in Arkansas, October, 1959.

miles. Had no one to play with except when they come out to the house."

He went on to tell us of how his mother had abandoned him in the woods when he was a baby. "Mother left me out in the woods in a pig house when I wasn't but six months old. Grandfather met mother in the woods and said, 'Where's that baby? If you haven't picked it up I'll blow both your heads off!' Grandfather took me up the hill, laid me on his bed. I never seen my mother again till after I was grown. Then she whipped me so much I was being scared of girls the rest of my life. But if you see a good cook, why, send 'em round here!" He laughed, and then fell still. "But my mother is no more kin to me than this lady here," he said, indicating me.

The mouthbow, or picking bow, looked like a hunting bow. Charlie put his mouth against the wood and plucked the string. "You work your mouth like you're singing a song, and you'll pick it. No, it don't make no difference what kind of wood you make it out of. Depends on the right kind of string. I had a little old can and I held it up beside there and it sounded twice as loud again. By Jude, I was the first one I ever knowed played one." The tone changed as he widened or narrowed his lips and he started up a tune. Neal began to call out dance steps, and we knew we had to record this unique sound.

"Have you got electricity here?" asked Alan.

"They run it out to the place, but I never had it connected," replied Charlie. "They want you to pay five dollars in advance, 'fraid you won't pay, by Jude! They ain't goin' to fool me!"

So, reluctant to drag out the huge batteries, we chose instead to drive Neal and Charlie to the motel where we were staying at near-by Mountain View. Charlie said he hadn't been there for years. "It's awful far, ain't it. I'd have to go afoot, and I'm crippled up, by Jude. I worked for the State all m'life—they wouldn't let nobody brand timber but me. Work? I did a bit of everything—made whiskey, ploughed corn on the hillside, planted cotton in the gravel. Used to carry mail—worn the hillside down carryin' mail! Had m'shoes break on me! I've made more whiskey than this room would hold. Made sugar whiskey, dollar a gallon. Now, by Jude, they have to give a dollar for half a pint! I tell you, the difference between now and fifty years ago is the difference between day and night."

We recorded on through the day, and when Alan put the earphones on Charlie so that he could listen to the play-back, he first looked apprehensive, then burst out laughing when he heard the mouthbow. "You'll play it over the radio and say it's a monkey, won't you!"

Now the night before, Jimmy, Alan and I had sung at a concert to raise funds for a local hospital, and Arkansas Senator Fulbright was there. He was staying at the same motel as us, and we invited him in to listen to the recordings. The two old men were quite overcome by his presence. Charlie was so flabbergasted that when the Senator, genuinely fascinated, asked him what the instrument was, said, "By Jude, I don't know!"

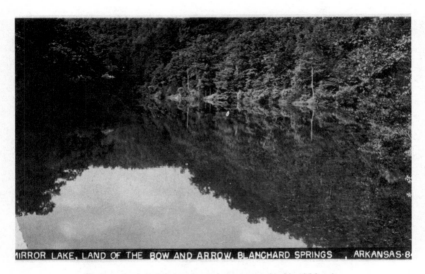

MIRROR LAKE, LAND OF THE BOW AND ARROW, BLANCHARD SPRINGS , ARKANSAS·8

The postcard of Arkansas given to me by Neal Morris.

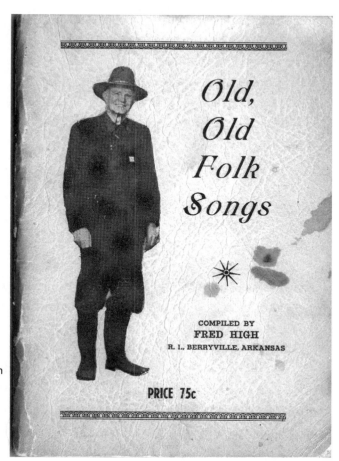

The collection of songs published by Fred High, of High, Arkansas, population 1.

I asked Charlie if he would kindly make me a bow. He simply handed me the one he was playing, saying it pleased him to think the bow would go back to England with me, because that's where his great-great granddaddy came from, and in any case, he could make another in half an hour. As we drove him back to his rosy wooden house, his two dogs, overjoyed to see him after his rare absence, jumped over the fence, leapt into the car and licked his face. "Whose dogs are these, by Jude? " he exclaimed.

I kept the bow as a souvenir, and Neal gave me a postcard of Mirror Lake, Blanchard Springs—"Land of the Bow and Arrow" autographed in his spidery hand. I also still have a copy of a book of Arkansas songs I bought printed by an independent character, Fred High, of High, Arkansas (Population 1), containing "73 songs, one for each of my years on earth", which still charms me with the eccentricity of its spelling.

When first to this countery a stringer I came
Acourting miss Sarro miss Sarro her name
So far-u-wel miss Sarro o ile bid U Adiew
I am a ruien for ever for the loving of you

This part of Arkansas is tornado country, and the day we drove away from Timbo, tornado warnings were being broadcast on the radio. It was the most dramatic sky I had ever seen, purple, green, yellow, orange and dark grey, with huge black clouds massing on the horizon, and the whole countryside lit by a lurid yellow light that was eerie and awesome. Thankfully the storm was at its worst elsewhere, but we were driving to a meeting with a singer whose life had been cruelly affected by a tornado.

We had been told by the folklorist John Quincey Wolf, who had spent years collecting in the Ozarks, that we should meet Almeda Riddle of Heber Springs. She was, in his opinion, the finest ballad singer in America, and when we heard her, Alan and I had to agree. She was a singer of such composure and quiet intensity, that you were compelled to listen. When she sang, for example, "The Merry Golden Tree", a British ballad of treachery on the high seas, and although it was one that I knew several variants of, it was as if I was hearing the story

Almeda Riddle

for the first time. There was such poignancy in Almeda's singing about the ocean when she'd never seen it in her life. In spite of this, when she sang, in her high, lonesome Ozark style, the refrain...

A-sailing on the low and lonesome low
Sailing on the lonely lowland sea

...she was able to convey the very essence of a lonely seascape. There was such clarity in her style, and she had that rare and admirable quality of serving the songs, rather than the songs serving her.

Almeda was a widow, having lost her husband some twenty-five years back in a tornado, and her face was scarred from injuries she received in one ten years before, when her house, with her in it, was picked up by the wind and set down again some distance away. She told of the tricks a tornado can play. The same wind that will pull a house up from its foundations and smash it to matchwood can whirl a hen-house to the top of a tree and leave it there, the hen still sitting and not an egg broken. It can bowl cars along like empty tin cans, and when a twister carried away the post office in Mountain View, one of the lost letters was mailed back from Northern Wisconsin, a distance of several hundred miles.

Many years back Almeda had written down in a book the words of all the songs she knew, and kept it in a box, but this too had been lost, blown away, and she said she never had the heart to write them out again. Luckily, she knew all her songs by heart—a remarkable feat as she knew many. It's a remarkable skill possessed by traditional singers, and some can even learn a song by hearing it just once.

Like the Morris family of Timbo, Almeda claimed personal connections to Frank and Jesse James: "I'm sure you've heard of Frank and Jesse James. Well, my father's grand-father and their father were brothers. I never was ashamed that the James boys was my cousins, but neither was I proud of it."

After my return to England, I kept in touch with Almeda for a while. On the following page is a transcription of the last letter she wrote to me (complete with misspellings). The original is reproduced opposite:

March 27 – 1960

Dear Shirly.

rec. yours sweet letter some days ago. but have been so busy just haunt goten around to ans it. thanks so much for writing. and thanks again for the nice things you said. I think you are a very wonderfull girl. and I did so enjoy the little while I was with you. — long enough to fall completely in love with you. I too hope we can meet again some time. and when I am not so up set. as I was that day. the elderly Lady I am nurseing now. is so very sweet and patient in her suffering it is almost a pleasure to care for her but do get tired and would love to Just go home and stay — have Friends visit me and have means to visit them do a little traveling here in the States to visit some Places I haunt seen. and some Friends I haunt seen for years.

Well maybe some time. if you come back to the U.S.A. and I am at all drop me a card to my home address and visit me there I get off and meet you there. we will stay just as long as you can. thanks for telling me about Alex. I have not doubted his Honesty at any time. I too think he is a very fine man. here is John G wolf address. ours,

he to is a very wonderfull man and I count him one of my closest and dearest friends. so by now this Pen is mısany
love always and write me again soon if you can.
Your friend
Al meda Riddell

Route 3, Box 122

Heber Springs, Ark.

March 27—1960

Dear Shirly

Rec. your sweet letter some days ago. But have been so buisy just haven't goten around to ans it. Thanks so much for writing and thanks again for the nice things you said. I think you are a very wonderfull girl, and I did so injoy the little while I was with you—long enough to fall completly in love with you. I too hope we can meet again sometime. And when I am not so upset as I was that day. The elderly lady I am nurseing now is so very sweet and patient in her suffering it is almost a pleasure to care for her but I do get tired and would love to just go home and stay, have freinds visit me and have means to visit them, do a little traveling here in the States to visit some places I havent seen, and some freinds I havent seen for years.

Well maybe some time. If you come back to the U.S.A. and can at all, drop me a card to my home address and visit me there. I get off and meet you there. We will stay just as long as you can. Thanks for telling me about Alin. I have not doubted his Honesty at any time. I too think he is a very fine man.....

So fly now this pen is so messy. Love always and write me again soon if you can

Your freind

Almeda Riddle

20

Hastings 1951
"Words, words, words" (Hamlet)

ONE EFFECT THE CINEMA HAD ON MY LIFE WAS THAT DOLLY and I fell in love with Laurence Olivier, and saw every film he made. Our favourites were *Wuthering Heights*, *Henry V* and *Hamlet*. So ardent were our feelings that we got the Shakespeare out and learned great passages of *Hamlet* by heart, and played a game called "Hamlet" every night in the big iron and brass bed that we shared. "I bags be Hamlet!" one of us would yell. "Oh, all right, I'll be Ophelia then," and off we'd go, trying to sound as much like Larry as possible. So besotted was I, that I used to think I *looked* like him as well and tried to imitate many of his facial expressions. That's probably responsible for a little scowl line I have between my eyes.

When I was fourteen or fifteen, and Dolly two years older, we went to London for a week to stay with Uncle George at his flat in Chelsea, and he knew where Laurence Olivier lived. We haunted the street, until, miraculously, our hero walked out of his front door. He noticed us across the road, and gave us a jaunty salute before getting into his car, at which Dolly burst into tears and I promptly followed suit. We went to see him in *Coriolanus*, managing to get cheap seats in the gods. I was so keyed up that when there was a pregnant pause in the play, and not then appreciating the dramatic power of silence, I thought he had forgotten his lines, and spent the rest of the evening in terror, hoping he wouldn't do it again!

Who would have thought that twenty-five years later I would actually talk to him. An invitation arrived out of the blue at my cottage, Red Rose, in Etchingham. It was from John Osborne the playwright, asking me to a garden party. And Laurence Olivier was there. I knew I'd never get another chance to speak to him, so very boldly I walked up and introduced myself. He was charming and affable and as I recall, giggled a bit. Or was that me? But such ease and charm had he that it was like talking to a favourite uncle.

The outcome of all this hero worship though was that my love of language grew; it stayed with me for life, and taught me to appreciate those often deceptively simple words of folksongs all the more.

21

Georgia Sea Island of St Simons

No more auction block for me
No more driver's lash for me
Nor more mistress call for me
Many thousands gone

THE DRIVE DOWN THROUGH ARKANSAS, MISSISSIPPI, ALABAMA and Georgia to reach our last destination of the field trip, St Simons, one of the Georgia Sea Islands, made me aware again how very far from England I was. I saw sights that I never would at home. There were fields full of cotton, snowy white and beautiful to look at, but so painfully thorny to pick. We took a day's sightseeing at the Okefenoke Swamp, we saw further KKK signs outside many towns, we ate, to my shame, in segregated restaurants, swam in segregated pools, and in Georgia we came across a convict chain-gang working at the side of the road. Alan stopped the car a short distance

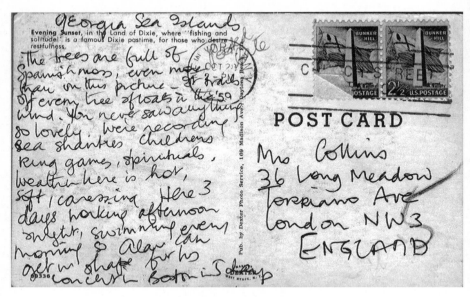

Postcard home from The Georgia Sea Islands.

away, got out with his camera and started taking pictures until he was spotted by the two guards. They ran towards us with their guns raised and told us to get moving. We moved. I wanted to get back to England alive. That evening, quite by chance, I read in a newspaper in our hotel in Savannah that the General Election had just taken place in Britain. To my dismay I saw that the Tories and Macmillan had won, and then to my delight a note about my home town: "High jinks in Hastings where ninety-one people voted for both candidates." I felt quite proud.

We had come to the Georgia Sea Islands to combine work and holiday, to get some rest before the long drive North back to New York. St Simons was possibly the most beautiful place I had seen in all my travels in America. All the trees, wide branching oaks, were hung with Spanish moss, pale misty grey-green, that trailed gently in the hot air, providing delicious shade. Whenever the breeze caught it, the moss lifted delicately and slowly. There was a sensual, caressing sense of languor that was so welcome after the hard work of the last few weeks.

It was Alan's plan that we should make our arrangements in the mornings, swim and relax in the afternoons, and record in the evenings. The sea was warm and surfy, the beaches of light golden sand with palms growing along the shore. We went to the beach at dawn one morning, waded in the pools and watched delighted as hundreds of fish leapt in and out of the water. The inland lakes and creeks, formed when the tide went out, were also full of fish, and their steep banks were black, which surprised me as the sand on the beach was so was very pale. When we got closer though, I could see that the banks were seething with millions of tiny black crabs!

It was a return visit for Alan. He had first recorded here in 1935 (the year I was born) with folklorists Zora Neale Hurston and Mary Elizabeth Barnicle. Their visit was still remembered, and we were greeted warmly by the islanders' leader, Big John Davis, who in the intervening twenty four years since he'd first met Alan, had travelled the world as a seaman, then returned to St Simons to live. It was a peaceful, relaxed place, and we were made very welcome.

Once the islands were the refuge of escaped slaves, and many of the people we met were their descendants. During the Civil War, St Simons was occupied by Union soldiers, and because many islanders joined their ranks to fight for freedom, much of the land was given to them when the War ended. Because of the relative isolation of the St Simons, (although white tourism was starting to encroach), this self-contained black community of fishermen and farmers were the keepers of music, song and dance handed down through generations. Bessie Jones, the finest woman singer there and a natural leader, had married an islander, bringing with her from her background in North Georgia a raft of songs and folklore from slavery times that she had learned from her grandparents, all four of whom had been slaves.

The music was superb, the conditions difficult. We were working in the evenings in the old school house, and Alan said it was worse than recording inside a barrel. For two nights we worked there, taking bottles of bourbon and crates of Coca Cola to keep everyone going. The nights were hot and sultry. One night, after we'd opened up the windows to let in some much-needed air, I counted the moths that flew in

The farmers and fishermen of the Georgia Sea Islands.

and settled, and gave up at over four hundred. Big John led the fishermen in shanties, and the fascinating "shouts", spirituals with a shuffling religious dance, with the movement instructions given in each line:-

Walk believer walk—O Daniel
Shout believer shout—O Daniel
Shout the Other Way—O Daniel
Give me that knee bone bend.
On the eagle wing—O Daniel
Fly I tell you fly—O Daniel
Rock believer rock—O Daniel
Give me that knee bone bend!

Bessie with the women and girls sang play-songs, ring-games and dances, and some rare and lovely spirituals. Their voices were full of character, individuality and warmth. They were people who obviously relished life, they laughed readily,

Big John Davis, The Georgia Sea Islands.

they were generous, warm and kind, and had such sweet and graceful manners that you felt blessed to be among them.

The morning we were due to leave, Big John came round to say goodbye. "Come back soon. The whole of St Simons is praying for you." It was a tearful farewell for us, leaving this idyll and heading back to the City. We needed their prayers, too, because we had just ten dollars to get the 800 or so miles back to New York, ten dollars to pay for food, overnight accommodation and road tolls. We'd got about two hundred yards along the road on the mainland when the radiator boiled over, and by the time we'd found a garage, it had burst. New pipe—five dollars! Then some twenty miles up the road it started to rain, heavy tropical rain which reduced the visibility to five yards. The windscreen wiper was having to work overtime—and then it fell off. We eventually found a Buick dealer, and the mechanic kindly mended it free, and off we headed for that evening's destination, Concord, North Caro-

Bessie Jones.

lina. We had an appointment at seven to meet J.E. Mainer, leader of a band, J.E. Mainer's Mountaineers, that had made commercial recordings in the 1930s on the RCS label. I argued with Alan about the wisdom of fitting one more visit in, but he said we were committed.

We congratulated ourselves when eventually we left the rain behind, but then hit some even more elemental weather in South Carolina, driving through a strange, bare land-scape, the road lined with trees blown almost parallel to the ground by a fearsome wind, and many more lying torn out by the roots. Then straight ahead of us we saw enormous dense black clouds, very low in the sky, seemingly just inches from the road's surface. We drove fast to get through them before the rain started; we entered them with our headlights full on, enveloped by the dark gloom, but we made it through, catching the rain just as we broke out. Were they still praying for us at St Simons? Were they singing one of my favourite songs of theirs, "Sheep, sheep, doncha know the road?"

We finally made it to Concord at eleven at night, hungry, tired and cold. The change in temperature from Georgia to North Carolina was incredible. It was chilly—and so was our reception from J.E. Mainer, understandably, as we were very late—not our fault, but still late. Amazingly, the band had decided to wait for us but they were none too happy. We set up quickly and recorded till half past one. At one point I asked J.E. what his initials stood for. He was still annoyed with us and wouldn't yield an inch. "Dunno," he said. "They just call me J.E." Twenty years back, he'd fallen out with his brother who'd signed a contract with a Northern record-ing company, a contract that excluded J.E. and they hadn't spoken to each other since. J.E.'s house was a big one, and we'd hoped he'd offer to put us up for the night, but for once American hospitality failed us. He bid us a cool good night, and we had to spend our last five dollars on a motel room. Remember, this was 1959, no credit cards, no cash points. Next morning, Alan wired his bank in New York for the last twenty-five dollars he had in his account and we waited until the authorisation came through.

We set off mid-morning and soon picked up a hitchhiker, a veteran travelling to Maryland. He told us his story. He'd been shelled in World War II, with injuries to his back and a foot, been in and out of hospital ever since, and was now going to hospital in Maryland to have his foot amputated. He'd sent his wife and son ahead by bus, but that had used up all his money. He showed us documents to back up the story, so Alan drove him all the way to the hospital, gave him ten dollars and wished him good luck. We were down to fifteen dollars. We drove on as far as the southern end of New Jersey, booked into a motel for the night, ready for the final stretch the next day. In the morning, when we entered the New Jersey Turnpike, we had three and a half dollars left. The toll was $2.95 to New York, the Holland Tunnel fifty cents.

We'd just driven onto the Turnpike and taken our ticket at the booth (you paid when you exited), when Alan said, "My God, we're almost out of gas! I don't think we can make it home!" The one credit card he did have was a Mobil gas (petrol) card, but Alan thought there wasn't a Mobil station on the Turnpike. Then he remembered we'd passed one just before the toll booth. In spite of the NO U-TURNS signs, Alan made a U-turn, and managed to do it right in front of a police car! The somewhat surprised cop signalled us to stop. Alan explained our predicament and I showed the officer our few coins. "Do you realise you're staring a fifteen dollar fine in the face?" he asked. But he kindly said he'd let us drive out to buy gas, but we'd have to pay $2.95 to exit the turnpike.

"We don't have a spare $2.95," said Alan. "Can we make another U-turn and try making it home?"

The officer's face flushed. "Do you realise you're staring a *thirty dollar* fine in the face?" But he saw the humour of the situation and relented. He strolled over to the clerk in the toll booth, had a brief word and Alan was allowed to walk out and get petrol in cans, fill up, make our U-turn north, and as we headed for home the patrolman gave us a pleasantly sardonic salute.

We made it safely back to New York, where we had all of two hours to spare before driving up to Boston, where we were appearing in concert with Sonny Terry and Brownie McGhee. Old friends of Alan's, I had met them in London a couple of years back, and they laughed and teased him when we told the story, but they were charming and easy company, and their music was as wonderful as ever. It was a successful concert, and we were paid in *cash*. We had enough money to stay in New England for a three-day break. We were exhausted and this was just what we needed. It was Fall, and breath-takingly beautiful, with the maple trees gold, red, orange and yellow. Huge orange pumpkins and apples filled the roadside stands, there were toffee apples, cider, freshly pressed apple juice, and above all the air was sweet, crisp and cold, so welcome after the dragging heat of the South.

22

Hastings 1952—Getting Closer

I LEFT SCHOOL AT SEVENTEEN, READY TO START TRAINING AS a teacher, my headmistress's suggestion. In the summer holiday, in order to earn some money, I took a job at a local Trade Union office, the MGWU. It was useful because I learned to type there, but since every letter started "Dear Sir and Brother" I found I couldn't take it very seriously. Still, the 27 shillings and 6 pence a week I was paid provided me with a green suit with a sun-ray pleated skirt which swished rather fetchingly I thought, and was at the same time sober enough to wear in class. I'd saved enough to buy my books and to pay my fare up to Furzedown College in Tooting Bec, South London.

This was a very trying time for me. I was homesick and had very little money. My Dad was supposed to send me a small weekly allowance, but it rarely came. I occasionally resorted to stealing a toothbrushful of Gibbs' Dentifrice or shakes of washing powder from other girls at the student hostel where I lived. I was ashamed of being poor and hated it. In any case, my heart wasn't in teaching. I stuck it for three terms, but it was having to do my first teaching practice on the Isle of Dogs in London that made me decide to quit. I was given a class of fifteen-year olds who were all getting ready to leave school and start work in the local industry—McDougall's flour factory. I was only eighteen, and they were far more worldly than I was and I didn't know *how* or *what* to teach them.

So I didn't go back to college after the first year. I worked as a bus conductress for the season in Hastings and stayed put. I rather enjoyed the work and it certainly had moments of fun. There was another temporary conductor, MacNamara, a young Irishman who sang a lot and generally had an air of whiskey about him and who livened the whole place up no end. I was travelling home from work one Sunday evening on his tram. As it stopped outside the Congregational Church, he swung round the pole, held up a hand to the queue and yelled, "Many are called, but few are chosen—I'll take four!"

We all hated getting the Bexhill run. Bexhill was posh, people there were wealthy and generally arrogant and rarely said "please" or "thank you". Some ladies were too delicate to give you their fares; they would drop their coins from their gloved hands into your palm as if to avoid contamination. I had to get a little revenge.

"I beg your pardon?" I asked one lady. "I didn't say anything," replied the customer. "Oh, I'm sorry", I said. "I thought you said thank you." It was petty, but reasonably satisfying.

We had to wrestle with long poles whenever the trolleys came off their overhead wires, a frequent occurrence at the busy Memorial, the Hastings town centre, where there was usually an audience ready to be entertained. The chivalrous among the male drivers would give you a hand, otherwise it was a bit like having a wobbly vaulting pole to manoeuvre, and often the crowd would give you a round of applause once the task was accomplished. We didn't much like being on early or late shifts, since this involved a long walk to or from the depot through three large and lonely parks. If you were on the early turn, you had the workmen's buses, and the top decks were dense with an almost impenetrable fug of cigarette smoke, there being an absolute resistance by the workmen to have the windows open.

By now, Dolly was set on being a composer, and she kept a bust of Beethoven, wild-haired and fiercely scowling, on the piano for inspiration. She was studying composition under Alan Bush at The Workers' Music Association at Paddington, and travelled up weekly from Hastings. We needed extra money to pay her fares, and when the summer was over, we all took various jobs to help out, preparing fruit and vegetables at Smedley's canning factory in Paddock Wood in Kent, hop-picking in the autumn, making artificial flowers at home in the winter.

This work just about kept us going, but it wasn't getting me any closer to fulfilling my ambition to be a singer. I had to make a move away from Hastings.

23

The Ending

For the roots they will wither
And the branches decay
He'll turn his back on you
And walk square away

Late November, 1959.
Letter to Peter Kennedy, English folklorist and friend:

> Dear Peter,
>
> We are in the middle of terribly hard times again.
> For the past week Alan has been in bed with a severe
> ear infection—in his good ear (he is half deaf in the
> other). I have been nursing him, but getting very little
> sleep—his groans at night are blood-curdling! I think
> he is improving, but we are both exhausted and scared
> to death he might lose his hearing altogether.

Alan has many prospects—but all in the future, which never seems to get any closer. And the biggest blow of all, Westminster Records has gone bankrupt. To make things worse, Alan had just finished dubbing his Italian tapes with them, so that's several hundred dollars' worth tied up—or lost. Alan is frantically trying to get the tapes back. On top of that, the girls who rented our apartment while we were away in the South left owing $150 rent, and they haven't paid the phone bill they ran up. Alan did manage to give his lecture in Detroit last week. While we were there an anthropologist played us some recent recordings he'd made of aborigines in Australia—their religious and magic customs. We heard an aboriginal spell for conjuring up the lightning god to strike your enemies—could do with it to use on the girls who did a bunk without settling up.

I'm longing for you to hear our field tapes—fantastic sounds—amazingly African from Mississippi, marvellous additions to the Child ballads from Arkansas—it all sounds so wonderful on stereo, too. Must finish now as I have to go and syringe Alan's ear. Life is so glamorous in the USA!

We spent the next few weeks editing our field-trip tapes, planning the albums, writing the notes. Our misfortunes weren't at an end. In mid-December we arrived home from a late-night broadcast at a New York radio station to find the road blocked by fire engines and the pizza parlour ablaze. The fire had spread up through the building and the firemen were fighting to get it under control. Alan was desperate, and tried to break through to rescue his precious, irreplaceable tapes and books, his life's work, but was restrained by the fire fighters. We just had to stand there and watch, praying that the fire would be contained before it reached the fifth floor. Miraculously, the flames didn't get past the fourth floor, and when Alan was at last allowed in, although he found considerable smoke and water damage, nothing of real importance lost. We boxed up all our possessions and moved out for a while. We were taken in by good friends Jean Ritchie and George Pickow until the place was habitable again after Christmas.

But the difficulties had taken their toll. I wrote home, "I don't think Alan and I are going to make it together. I'll probably be home in January."

And that's how it ended. Alan felt he wanted to be on his own, that he couldn't commit himself permanently to our relationship, and that I should return to England. A passage was booked for me on the SS France and on a bitterly cold and snowy January day, I left New York and Alan. It was a stormy passage home across the Atlantic, with huge seas through the Bay of Biscay, waves so high that they towered over the liner as it went down into the troughs. It all seemed rather fitting to me.

Mum and Dolly were there to greet me at Waterloo Station (the terminus of the line from Southampton Docks) at the end of my journey, and it was wonderful to see them, and to be home in England again. I was proudly wearing a white floor-length mock-sheepskin coat, the like of which probably hadn't been seen in London. On reflection, I think I must have looked like a Yeti!

C

121 West 3rd St.,
New York City, 12,
Jan. 26, 1960.

To whom it may concern:

    This letter authorizes Miss Shirley Collins to act as my agent in arranging BBC broadcasts for the 3rd program , based on the tapes made in the South during the summer of 1959. She has a demonstration txpxx set of tapes with her and may use them to show what the material would be like. A ten percent agent's commission will be paid to her out of my fees for the broadcasts.
    She is also authorized to arrange in her own behalf to use the tapes from last summer, including the demonstration tapes she has with her, as material for boradcasts on Light or Home, on the BBC, or as material for lectures on the trip this summer. Provided always that previous to the broadcasts the agreed on fees are set up for the performers and the copyright of the numbers are carefully seen to.   All other fees from such broadcats in Britan to go to Miss Co.
    The demonstration tapes are to be returned to Mr. Lomax on request, and none of the material is to be copied for recording purposes, for archive purposes or to be published in any way without written permission from Mr. Lomax.

    Miss Collins also has my permission to negotiate for the sale of these recordings with the BBC Permanent record library, with a ten percent commission for any sales made.

    Accepted and agreed

    Shirley Collins

    Shirley E. Collins

Alan Lomax

Alan's letter authorising me to act as his agent in the UK after my return to England, 1960.

I missed Alan dreadfully, but I was young and resilient and picked up the threads in England again. The Folk Revival was getting under way, folk clubs flourishing all over the country, and I was able to make a living as a singer. Within a few months or so I met the designer Austin John Marshall,

Alan and me on holiday in Majorca, 1960.

who was doing the artwork for three HMV compilation folk albums on which I had a couple of tracks.

When the news reached Alan of this friendship he came over to England in the summer of 1960 and asked me to marry him. We flew off to Majorca, a peaceful place then, to talk things over, staying in a tiny pensione opposite the island of Dragonera, to which we swam every day and sun-bathed on the rocks. We ate rough country bread spread thickly with apricot preserve for breakfast, and fresh-caught fish with garlic and tomatoes doused with heavy olive oil for dinner. But even in that paradise there were anxieties for me. Alan had told me stories about his time collecting in Spain, how often he had been under the watchful and baleful glare of the Guardia Civil. In Majorca, we had surrendered our passports, as you had to by law, to the pensione owners, so I knew they could tell that we weren't married. Every night I dreaded a knock on the door from the fascist police. As it happened, none came of course. The world was a far more sophisticated and tolerant place than I imagined it to be. The highlights of the holiday were our visits to Alan's friend, Robert Graves among the lemon groves of Deya. How moved I was by the sight of those two noble heads together—they looked like statues from the classical world come to life, or Minotaurs perhaps. Fanciful girl! Robert mentioned the visits in his diaries, dated July 31st and August 6th, 1960... 'Alan Lomax came and sang.... and his friend Shirley of Sussex....' I visited Robert Graves in London just once or twice more over the next couple of years, taking my baby daughter Polly in her carry-cot to one of his parties.

It was an idyllic time together in Majorca, but even so, I couldn't accept Alan's offer of marriage—it was too late. He'd rejected me twice, and I didn't trust this change of heart, although I loved him still. In any case, I wanted to live in England. As it turned out, Alan married for the second time in 1961, the same year I married Austin John.

We had two children, Polly Elizabeth and Robert Austin Frederick born one year, one month, one week and one day apart. Polly, Rob, and my grandsons Joe and Louis, are the people I love best in this world, and I never regretted my decision.

I continued my singing career after the children were born, performing as and when my duties as a mum would allow while the children were little. Between 1955 and 1963 I'd appeared on three compilation LPs and I'd made five solo EPs of British and Appalachian songs. Then in 1964, at the instigation of Austin John, I teamed up with the avant-garde guitarist Davy Graham, recording the album *Folk Roots, New Routes*. I sang a mix of English and Appalachian songs; the American influence was still there. With Davy's blend of jazz, Indian and North African styles, the eclecticism of his arrangements created quite a stir. It was an interesting experiment, but not one that I wanted to pursue. I was determined to focus on English songs and to find a more appropriate way of accompanying them. It was at this point that my sister Dolly and I decided to join forces, with Dolly as arranger and accompanist. The union got off to a bit of a rocky start though, as Dolly chose to write her first arrangement for three French horns!

We had grown to love Early Music through Uncle Fred's enthusiasm for it, and while attending a rehearsal of Michael Morrow's group Musica Reservata around 1966, discovered our ideal instrument, the flute-organ. Made by Noel Mander, it

Shortly after my
return to England.

was an exquisite reproduction of a 17th century portative pipe
organ—perfect because of its breathy and airy fluting notes.
We recorded with it for the first time on our 1967 album *The
Sweet Primeroses*, followed in the same year by *The Power of
the True Love Knot*, produced by Joe Boyd. There were three
additional musicians, the exuberant duo Robin Williamson
and Mike Heron of the Incredible String Band, and Bram
Martin playing his 1740 Tosturi cello. All the material was
English, with the exception of one Appalachian ballad which
I couldn't resist including.

We were in the right place at the right time in 1969 when EMI were setting up the Harvest label to record artists outside the mainstream of popular music. Austin John convinced Harvest that Dolly and I should record for them, with him as producer. We had recently met David Munrow, the blazing young genius of Early Music and he agreed to be Musical Director for our first Harvest album, *Anthems in Eden*. Side one of *Anthems* was an ambitious song-cycle, a suite of English folk songs arranged by Dolly for period instruments, and a group of David's musicians from his Early Music Consort (but dubbed "Dolly Collins' Harmonious Sweet England Band" for the album) played rebecs, sackbuts, crumhorns and violones, with Christopher Hogwood on harpsichord. We did a few live performances of *Anthems*, including one for Radio 2, and then Dolly and I toured as a duo with the flute-organ, appearing at folk clubs and universities, and at The Queen Elizabeth Hall and the Royal Albert Hall. Our second album for Harvest, *Love, Death and the Lady* followed, a far more sombre album, reflecting the difficulties of the ending of my marriage to Austin John.

After the divorce, the children and I moved away from London to the Sussex countryside to Red Rose, a Tudor cottage I rented in the village of Etchingham. It was from here that I later married Ashley Hutchings, bassist with Fairport Convention and Steeleye Span, and here, too, that we formed The Albion Country Band, the name we gave the twenty-six musicians from the genres of folk, early music and rock who played on my album *No Roses*.

During the time of the power cuts and the short-working week Britain in 1974, we formed an acoustic band with Sussex musicians Terry Potter and Ian Holder—an idea of

Martin Carthy's. We called it the Etchingham Steam Band. It was modest, but proved very popular, and it lasted for two years. We often played for dancing, country dancing, and when the Etchinghams ran out of steam, and the country's electricity supply became more reliable again, we started Albion up again as the Albion Dance Band. As on *No Roses*, this crusading band had elements of folk rock, early music and traditional folk music. In its mighty line-up were Simon Nicol of Fairport Convention, Dave Mattacks and Mike Gregory on drums, Phil Pickett, leader of the New London Consort and master of every medieval wind instrument, John Sothcott of St George's Canzona on vielle, Graeme Taylor, electric guitar, John Tams, melodeon and vocals, John Rodd, concertina, and Eddie Upton, our caller and vocalist. Ashley, was on electric bass and I sang. We played hugely enjoyable social dances where people flocked onto the floor swept along by this big, beautiful and unique sound, the music adding strength and vitality to dances that ranged from the 14th to the 19th centuries. We recorded the album *The Prospect Before Us* in 1976 and worked at the National Theatre in two productions, *The Mysteries* and *Lark Rise*.

But the lure of the theatre and all that it held was irresistible to Ashley. He left Red Rose to live in London with an actress. Husband and band were lost in one fell swoop. Dolly and I started to work together again, and we made an album for Topic in 1978, *For As Many As Will*, but it was to be our swansong. I divorced Ashley in 1980, but the outcome of it all was that I had lost confidence and my voice began to fail me. I persevered for a couple of years, but I felt very keenly that I was no longer doing justice to the music I loved so much. My nerve had gone. I took some consolation in the fact that my

THE ASSOCIATION FOR CULTURAL EQUITY
AT HUNTER COLLEGE

Alan Lomax & Conrad Arensberg, Co-Directors
A Global Study of Expressive Behavior

Global Jukebox
Cantometrics & Choreometrics
American Patchwork Television Series

450 West 41st Street, 6th Floor
New York City, NY 10036
Tel: (212) 268-4623
Fax: (212) 279-3710

[handwritten letter]

Letter from Alan sent to me in the late eighties.

"Dearest Friend, I'm sending you the debut edition of the Atlantic set, along with the book they were published to celebrate. Forgive me for this tardiness. I'm overtaxed and a bit on the weary side. Still thinking of you often and fondly. Alan."

career had lasted over twenty-five years, and had taken me all over the world singing in venues that ranged from humble top-rooms of pubs, to the grandest of halls—from The Royal Oak, Lewes, to the Opera House, Sydney.

I was also struggling financially. Polly had won a place at Oxford University at St Edmund Hall, the first ever member of our family to go to University, Rob was at 6th form college, and I was their sole support. I commuted between Sussex and London working in a literary agency for two years, then moving to a job that I really loved at the British Museum book-shop. But all the while I felt that the real Shirley Collins had vanished, and when I was offered a post as Public Relations Officer for The English Folk Dance and Song Society at Cecil Sharp House, I felt it was my chance to get back to folk music. I shouldn't have listened to their blandishments.

When I started work, it became clear that I had been deceived; the work was secretarial, and the unfriendly atmos-phere at Cecil Sharp House hadn't improved much since the 1950s. After six months I quit, and left London for good. A post of "folk animateur" was being offered in Sussex by South East Arts. I took the job and ran The Wealden Folk Project for eighteen months. I was dismayed to run up against a lack of interest in, and even worse, a prejudice against, the music of England. When I approached the music officer for Sussex schools to discuss how we could put Sussex traditional music into the local schools, I was told that they already had a full programme of folk music. When I pressed further, he explained that there was a Gamelan orchestra and a West Indian steel band, and that there wasn't room for anything else. Why wasn't I surprised? All my working life had been a struggle to promote English music. But it still begs the question—why do the English yield and relinquish their own culture so willingly? When my tenure of The Wealden Folk Project came to an end, I worked for Oxfam in Brighton for nearly three years.

CB80

Then, in 1990, my renaissance started with a visit from the musician David Tibet; he told me he had been a great admirer of my work for many years, and felt that my recordings should be made available. He released *A Fountain of Snow*, a compilation CD of twenty-four of my Topic recordings on his own Durtro label in 1991, followed by *Harking Back* in 1998, an album of live concert recordings of Dolly and me in Dublin.

Next, David Suff of Fledg'ling Records took up the cause, and reissued many of my deleted albums, culminating in *Within Sound*, a 4-CD box-set retrospective, released in 2003. and *Snapshots* in 2006.

In 1997, Rounder Records in the States released *Southern Journey*, a 12-CD collection of the music Alan and I had recorded in 1959, along with a solo CD by Fred McDowell, *The First Recordings*. I was delighted to see on every album cover a photograph I'd taken of Alan in Virginia, sitting with earphones on, listening with rapt concentration to his recordings of Uncle Wade Ward. The reissues created a lot of interest, and it was at this point that Malcolm Taylor of the Vaughan Williams Memorial Library invited me to give an illustrated talk there about the experience, and this kickstarted a modest new career as a lecturer. But I believe that David Tibet, David Suff and Malcolm Taylor restored me to my true self, and I'm still very touched by the faith they had in me and my music, and feel fortunate to have the friendship of three such honourable people.

The *America Over the Water* talk has grown into a full show with contemporaneous pictures added to the sound of the wonderful 1959 field recordings, and the dramatic impact of it all strengthened by actor Pip Barnes' performances of many of the American characters that I met all that time ago in 1959.

I must mention my friendship with Pip. I met him in 1978 at a farewell party given at The National Theatre on the last night of *Lark Rise*, where I was thankful to be seeing the back of theatre life and all the anguish it had caused me. It's remarkable how life changes again. I liked the look of Pip instantly, and when we talked, he said he had often been in the audience at The Albion Dance Band gigs, and had envied Ashley dancing with me. I boldly gave him my phone number, and said if he was ever visiting Bexhill where I lived at the time, he'd be most welcome.

But why would a handsome young actor want to visit Bexhill-on-Sea? It had an elderly population, and was full of shops that catered for them. One had a sign in the window that said, 'OUR CHANGING ROOMS ARE NICE AND WARM', and another, 'ON PARLE FRANCAIS—FRIDAYS ONLY'. A typical headline in *The Bexhill Observer* read: 'Bexhill resident dies suddenly aged 89'. But a few days later Pip whizzed down on his motor scooter. We went to a local pub, discovered a shared love of Shakespeare, and started a passionate relationship that lasted a good few years, although I was nearly twenty years his senior (about the same difference in reverse as there was between Alan and me). It eventually and inevitably changed, but was never lost, growing into a deep friendship. We started a conversation twenty-eight years ago that shows no sign of coming to an end, and now we appear in the *America Over the Water* show together, and that makes me very happy indeed.

My home is now in Lewes, the beautiful county town of Sussex, where I live happily in a Victorian cottage hard by the Castle. Alan, I think, would have appreciated the fact that between 1768 and 1774, Lewes was home to Thomas Paine, author of *Rights of Man* and *The Age of Reason*. Paine went to America in October 1774, and within two years had written his pamphlet *Common Sense* in which he called for independence from the English crown. George Washington said that he was persuaded of the rightness of this cause after reading Paine's work, and believed that Paine was... "one of the greatest of all the forces that brought about, sustained and carried to a successful conclusion the American War of Independence." Paine was also the man who coined the phrase "United States of America".

I met Alan just once more in my life when he came to see me in the early 1990s. The warmth and affection between us was still there, the attraction still strong. He talked passionately about his hugely ambitious project "Cantometrics", a system he devised to classify song style on a global scale. He said the work was exhausting him, but that he felt driven. We argued hotly about who we considered to be the greatest ballad singer, and we talked fondly about old times together. I felt quite a pang as I waved him goodbye at Brighton Station the following morning. It was the last time I saw him.

I never quite lost my affection or my regard for Alan, and he apparently retained some feeling for me over the years, for in 1993 he sent me a copy of his book *The Land Where the*

Blues Began. He had inscribed it: "With much love and great admiration to one of the sweetest singers and ladies who ever walked and graced the green ways of this earth."

And now I can return the compliment:

Passionate about traditional music and the lives of working people, Alan Lomax was their champion. His legacy is the books that he wrote, and the thousands of field recordings that he made.

But when you're on some distant shore
Think on your absent friend
And when the wind blows high and clear
A line or two pray send
And when the wind blows high and clear
Pray do send it, love, to me
That I shall know by your hand-write
How times have gone with thee

Appalachian folk song

Appendices

SHIRLEY COLLINS
A SELECTED DISCOGRAPHY

The first year given is that of the CD re-issue of the album.
Dolly Collins is featured on the albums marked *; those
specifically credited to Shirley and Dolly Collins are marked **.

All CDs with NEST and FLED prefixes are on Fledg'ling Records
and are available from them at www.thebeesknees.com

For a more detailed discography,
please visit www.shirleycollins.co.uk

2006:   SNAPSHOTS * (FLED 3057)
          Live concert performances from the 1970s and demo
          recordings from the 1960s. 22 tracks, 12 previously
          unreleased.

2003:   WITHIN SOUND * (NEST 5001)
          Comprehensive 4-CD box set overview of Shirley and
          Dolly's career, including many previously unreleased
          tracks, and extensive notes and photographs in the
          book included within.

2004:   NO ROSES * Castle Music (CMRCD951)
With The Albion Country Band.
Originally released B&C 1971

2003:   LOVE, DEATH & THE LADY ** (FLED 3039)
Originally released EMI 1970

2001:   FALSE TRUE LOVERS (FLED 3029)
Originally released Folkways 1960

2000:   THE POWER OF THE TRUE LOVE KNOT *
(FLED 3028) Originally released Polydor 1967

1999:   FOLK ROOTS, NEW ROUTES (TSCD 819)
With Davy Graham. Originally released Decca 1964

1999:   SWEET ENGLAND (TSCD 815)
Originally released Decca 1959

1999:   ADIEU TO OLD ENGLAND * (FLED 3023)
Originally released Topic 1974

1998:   HARKING BACK ** (DURTRO 046CD)

1995:   THE ETCHINGHAM STEAM BAND (FLED 3002)

1995:   THE HOLLY BEARS THE CROWN * (FLED 3006)
Credited to "The Young Tradition with Shirley and Dolly
Collins"

1995:   THE SWEET PRIMEROSES * (TSCD 476)
Originally released Topic 1967

1994:   FOR AS MANY AS WILL ** (FLED 1003)
Originally released Topic 1978

1993:   ANTHEMS IN EDEN ** (CDEMS 1477)
Originally released EMI 1969

1993:   THE PROSPECT BEFORE US (CDEMS 1476)
With The Albion Dance Band. Originally released EMI
1977

1992:   FOUNTAIN OF SNOW * (DURTRO 010CD)

DISCOGRAPHY OF THE 1959 RECORDINGS

Atlantic Records LP releases, 1960:
  Sounds Of The South, SD-1346
  Blue Ridge Mountain Music, SD-1347
  Roots Of The Blues, SD-1348
  White Spirituals, SD-1349
  American Folk Songs For Children, SD-1350
  Negro Church Music, SD-1351
  The Blues Roll On, SD-1352

The preceding seven albums were also packaged in a set as:
  "Southern Folk Heritage", HS-1 and SCHS-1, 1960.

This complete collection was then released as:
  "Sounds of the South", 4 CD Box Set, 1993, Atlantic Records,
  #82496

Prestige International's Documentary Series LP releases, 1961:
  "Southern Journey" 12 vol. series. Prestige 25001-25012.
  Southern Journey 1: Georgia Sea Islands, Volume 1, INT-25001
  Southern Journey 2: Georgia Sea Islands, Volume 2, INT-25002
  Southern Journey 3: Ballads and Breakdowns from the
  Southern Mountains, INT-25003
  Southern Journey 4: Banjo Songs, Ballads and Reels from the
  Southern Mountains, INT-25004
  Southern Journey 5: Deep South... Sacred and Sinful, INT-25005
  Southern Journey 6: Folk Songs from the Ozarks, INT-25006

Southern Journey 7: All Day Singing from "THE SACRED HARP", INT-25007

Southern Journey 8: The Eastern Shores, INT-25008

Southern Journey 9: Bad Man Ballads, INT-25009

Southern Journey 10: Yazoo Delta Blues and Spirituals, INT-25010

Southern Journey 11: Southern White Spirituals, INT-25011

Southern Journey 12: Honor the Lamb: The Belleville A Capella Choir of the Church of God and Saints of Christ, INT-25012

SOUTHERN JOURNEY - THE ALAN LOMAX COLLECTION

New series released by Rounder Records 1997

http://www.rounder.com

THE ALAN LOMAX COLLECTION SAMPLER (CD 1700)

FRED MCDOWELL: THE FIRST RECORDINGS (CD 1718)

Vol 1:	VOICES FROM THE SOUTH (CD 1701)
Vol 2:	BALLADS & BREAKDOWNS (CD 1702)
Vol 3:	61 HIGHWAY MISSISSIPPI (CD 1703)
Vol 4:	BRETHREN, WE MEET AGAIN (CD 1704)
Vol 5:	BAD MAN BALLADS (CD 1705)
Vol 6:	DON'TCHA KNOW THE ROAD (CD 1706)
Vol 7:	OZARK FRONTIER (CD 1707)
Vol 8:	VELVET VOICES (CD 1708)
Vol 9:	HARP OF 1000 STRINGS (CD 1709)
Vol 10:	AND GLORY SHONE AROUND (CD 1710)
Vol 11:	HONOR THE LAMB (CD 1711)
Vol 12:	GEORGIA SEA ISLANDS (CD 1712)
Vol 13:	EARLIEST TIMES (CD 1713)

COMPLETE RECORDING LOGS
FROM THE 1959 SOUTHERN
COLLECTING TRIP

The following pages reproduce Alan Lomax's recording logs of the 1959 field trip.

T-844-927

This is the CARBON

SUMMER 1959

AUGUST 24, 1959

REEL NO:	PERFORMER:	TITLE:	ADDRESS	TIME
1.1.	Texas Gladden	Dark Blue Eyes	Salem, Va. Route? Box 497	
2.2.	Hobart Smith	Railroad Bill (Distorted)	106 Doke St. Bluefield Phone: 2-2624/2-0125	
1.3.	Hobart Smith	Peg and Awl		2.10
1.4.	Hobe, Texas & Preston Smith	Lonely Tombs		2.35
1.5.	"	When the Stars Begin to Fall (good tune)		4.20
1.6.	"	Jim and Me		2.25
1.7.	Hobe Smith	Drunken Hiccups -fiddle solo XX		3.45
1.8.	Hobe Smith	John Brown(dreamt the Devil was dead) Fiddle		1.45
~~1.9.~~	~~Texas Gladden~~	~~Am I Born to Die~~		
1.10	Hobe Smith	I'm Going Down the Road Feeling Bad		

AUGUST 24, 1959. T-845

REEL NO:	PERFORMER:	TITLE:	ADDRESS	TIME
2.1.	Hobe Smith	I'M Goin' Down the Road (banjo;guit)		
2.2.	Hobe Smith	Dixie(piano) X		
2.3.	"	Cindy (piano) XX		
2.4.	"	Fly Around my Blue-Eyed Girl (piano)XXX		
2.5.	Texas Gladden	Dark Scenes of Winter X		
2.6.	"	I Never Will Marry (noisy)*		
2.6.	"	Interview-on elopement X		
2.7.	"	I Never Will Marry (take 2)		1.55
2.8.	"	Interview/and Poem		
2.9.	"	Poem:"Meditation "		
2.10	"	Hick's Farewell. X		
2.11.	"	Three Little Babes XXX		
2.12.	Hobart Smith	Hawkins County Jail (song)		

August 25th 1959 at Bluefield, Va.   T-846

REEL NO:	PERFORMER:	TITLE:	ADDRESS:	TIME:
3.1.	Hobe Smith	Poor Ellen Smith(with banjo) Y		2.00
3.2.	Texas Gladden	Cold Mountains X		1.15
3.3.		Brisk Young Soldier XX (Broken Token)		1.45
3.4.	Hobe Smith	The Arkansas Traveler (banjo)XXX		1.55
3.5.	"	Banging Breakdown (banjo)XXX		1.30
3.6.	"	Black Annie (banjo)X false start		1.50
3.7.	"	Graveyard Blues (guitar) XX		3.15
3.8.	"	See That My Grave is Kept Clean X (guitar) plus good interview		3.20
3.9.	"	Claud Allen (guitar) X		3.15
3.10	"	Soldier, Soldier (guitar)XXX		1.40
3.11.	"	Little Schoolboy (2 Brothers)		4.05

T-847

Bluefield, Va, August 25th, 1959. Cut low frequency hum.

REEL NO:	PERFORMER:	TITLE:	ADDRESS:	TIME:
4.1.	Hobe Smith	Parson Burrs (guitar)X XXX (Will aggravate your souls)		2.15
4.2.	"	Brownskin Blues (guitar-wonderful)XXX		2.50
4.3.	"	Railroad Bill (guitar)XXXX		3.00
4.4.	"	Billy in the Low Ground X (fiddle - lovely sound)		2.00
4.5.	"	Old Joe Clark (fiddle-fabulous) XXXX		
4.6.	"	Sourwood Mt. (fiddle) XX .		

August 26th, Salem, Va.

REEL NO:	PERFORMER:	TITLE:	ADDRESS:	TIME:
4.7.	Texas Gladden	Whole Heapa Little Horses XXXX		
4.8.	"	The Dapple Cow (lullabye -new)-XX / The Teddy Bears' Picnic (with baby)		
4.9.	"	Whole Heapa little Horses		
4.10	"	Lone Green Valley		
4.11.	"	The Gipsy Davy		

REEL:	PERFORMER:	TITLE:	ADDRESS:	TIME:
8.1.	Wade Ward (67) banj / Charlie Higgins (81) fiddle / Dave Poe (36) guit.	Little Maggie / "(bad mix ?)" / "	Independence, Va. / Route 2, Galax, Va. / Phone. Belmont, 6-2006 / Independence, Va.	
5.2.	same 3	Cripple Creek		
5.3.	"	Willow Garden XXXX		
5.4.	"	Uncle Charley's Breakdown XXXX (own composition)		
5.5.	"	Paddy on the Turnpike XXXX		1.45
5.6.	"	Don't Let Your Deal Go Down		.45
5.7.	"	Walking In my Sleep (vocal Dave Poe)		1.15
5.8.	"	?		
5.9.	George Stoneman	Cindy (banjo solo) Route 30, Box 53		1.10
5.10.	" (76)	Sally Anne (" ")XX Galax, Va.		1.30
5.11.	"	Ida Red (2 ")XX		1.15
5.12.	Norman Edmonds -fid 70 / Paul Edmonds-guit 36 / Rufus Quesinberry-banj 58	Walking in the Parlor - Route 2,Hillsville / Woodlawn, Va. / Woodlawn, Va.		1.45
5.13.	same 3	Sally Anne		2.20
5.14.	Norman Edmonds	Bonaparte's Retreat fiddle Solo		1.40
5.15.	group	Breaking Up Christmas XXXX		1.55
5.16.	"	Salt River		1.50

6.1.	same group	Greasy String XX (lovely tune, good playing stereo - medium tempo)		
6.2.	"	Lonesome Dove XX		

-cont -

TAPE:	PERFORMER:	TITLE:	ADDRESS:	TIME:
6.2.	George Stoneman -banjo / Glen Stoneman -fiddle	Silly Bill -lvdy X (with James Lindsay-guit)	Route 30, Galax.	
.6.4.	"	Leather Breeches X (with Cullen Gallyen-guit)		1.05
6.5.	"	John Henry X - lively (with Lindsay-guit)		2.40
6.6.	"	Richland (2"")X		1.15
6.7.	"	Fortune (""")X		
6.8.	"	Cindy (" ")X		

The Mt. Ramblers: (38)

6.9.	James Lindsay(guit & mand) / Cullen Gelyen (banjo -20)	Jesse James XXX (as dance tune;bass too heavy;?banjo)	Route 4, Galax, / Route 1, Box 51, Low Gap, N.C.	2.10
	Charles Hawkes (banjo -30)		Route 2, Box 170, Galax.	
	Eldridge Montgomery(guit)28	....	Route 4, Galax.	
	Thurman Pugh(bass -24)	....	Route 2, Fries, Va.	

Little Liza Jane (lovely tune;left side muffled)

6.10	group			
6.11.	"	Old Joe Clark (Galyen fiddle)x×x×x		.50
6.12.	"	Shady Grove		2.20
6.13.	Ruby Vass ..	Sinful to Flirt (....Route 1, Box 83 "with guitar")	Hillsville, Va.)	

T-850

7.1.	Ruby Vass.	Banks of the Ohio XXX		2.35
7.2.	"	The Old Gospel Ship XXX		2.55
7.3.	"	Single Girl		2.10
7.4.	Mt. Ramblers	Shady Grove (Thyman Pugh vocal)		
7.5.	"	Shady Grove -take 2. XX		

7.6. Recorded at later date:
Baptism at Huntsville, Ala. Remarks by visiting Birmingam minister,

7.7. A Long-Metre Hymn from same church.

TAPE: T-853
AUGUST 31st, 1959 at Hillsville, Va.

PERFORMER:	TITLE:
10.1. Wade Ward / Charlie Higgins / Bob Carpenter-guit.	Joe Clark
10.2. Piney Woods Gal	Piney Woods Gal
10.3. "	Sally Anne
10.4. "	Backstep Cindy.
10.5. "	June Apple.
10.6. Wade Ward / Bob Carpenter	Chilly Winds (banjo & guit)
10.7. " "	Old Joe Clarke (banjo and guit)
10.8. Charlie Higgins / Bob Carpenter	Katy Hill (fiddle and guit.)
10.9. Charlie Higgins / Bob Carpenter	Blackberry Blossom (fiddle and guit)
10.10.	Katy Hill (2"") or: East Tennessee Blues
10.11.	?
A 10.12.	Wildwood Flower (vocal:Carpenter)

T-854
August 1st, Rugby, Va. Inserted on this tape altho the recd later)

PERFORMER:	TITLE:
A 11.1. Estil & Orna Ball	Paper of Pins Grassy Creek. N.C.
11.2. Estil, and Lacey Richardson	Tribulations (2 guitars;2 vocal)
Back to Galax:	
11.3. Bob Carpenter	Big Ball in Brooklyn
A 11.4. Wade Ward	Chilly Winds (solo banjo)
11.5. " "	Old Joe Clark
11.6. " "	Chick Old Hen cttle On
11.7. " "	Molly Put the Kettle On

-cont -

TAPE: T-851
Sunday, August 29th, Hillsville, Va.

PERFORMER:	TITLE:	ADDRESS:	TIME:
8.1. Mt. Ramblers	Cotton-Eye Joe (Cullen Galyen-vocal)		2.25
8.2. "	Take 2.		
A 8.3. "	Take 3. (O.K.) XXXXX		2.00
8.4. "	John Henry (Eldridge Montgomery-vocal)		
8.5. "	Take 2 XXXX " OK		
A 8.6. "	Rosewood Casket XXX (Montgomery -vocal)		
A 8.7. "	Silly Bill - breakdown XX		2.25
A 8.8. "	Big Tilda O breakdown XXXXX		2.10
A 8.9. "	Big Ball in Boston (Thyman Pugh-vocal) arr. Lindsay		2.10
8.10 "	Take 2.		
A 8.11 "	Take 3 -- OK XX		2.15.

T-852

PERFORMER:	TITLE:		
A 9.1. "	The Hickory Cane XXXXX (Pugh vocal) good-must be spliced)		
A 9.2. "	John Henry.XX (Galyen - vocal)		
9.3.	Pretty Polly (Eldridge - vocal)		3.55.
9.4. Wade Ward	Joe Clarke (with bass-Bob Carpenter)XX (and chopped manufacturer) Galyen, guitar.)		
9.5. Mt. Ramblers.	The Old Country Church XXXX (and chopped manufacturer) (Pugh -vocal)		
A 9.6. "	My Lord Keeps a Record (2"") XXXX (end vocal) 3.30 XXX Padre end fist		
A 9.7. "	Baptising Down at the Creek ("XXXX Padre end fist		
9.8.	Uncle Joe - Bid (not rough the Closely Good) Old Joe Clark XXXX	Box 74, Independe Va.	
9.9. Ward, Higgins, Bob Carpenter-guit Interview. Tunes, local fiddlings + talk	Interview with Charlie Higgins, and talk.... how Uncle Charlie learned to play.		
9.10. Wade Ward-banjo / Cullen Galyen-guit / Carpenter - bass.			

TAPE:	PERFORMER:	TITLE:	ADDRESS:
11.8.	Wade Ward	Cumberland Gap	
11.9.	"	Reuben Train	
11.10.	"	John Henry	
11.11.	"	Fox Chase (hounds by Bob Carpenter)	
11.12.	"	Chilly Winds (slightly out of tune)	

T-955

TAPE:	PERFORMER:	TITLE:	ADDRESS:
12.1.	Charlie Higgins Bob Carpenter	Grey Eagle	
12.2.	Bob Carpenter	The Wildwood Flower	
12.3.	"	Kenny Wagoner	
12.4.	"	The Burglar Man.	

At Rugby, Va.

TAPE:	PERFORMER:	TITLE:	ADDRESS:
12.5.	Estil Ball (g.voc) Blair Reedy (voc) Lacey Richardson (gu.voc)	Tribulations XYXXX all: Grassy Creek. N.C. own comp.	
12.6.	Estil Ball -guit;voc Blair Reedy-guit-voc	When I Get Home I'll XYXXX Be Satisfied own comp. Pub:Starbright Co.Madison,Tenn.	
12.7.	Estil & Blair	Take 2	
12.8.	Estil & Lacey	Please Let me Stay Longer XYXXY both guitar and vocal own comp.	
12.9.	Estil	Pretty Polly YXXXY	
22.10.	Estil	Ellen Smith. XXXXY	
12.11.	Estil	Father, Jesus Loves You.	
12.12.	Estil	His announcement.	

T-856

TAPE:	PERFORMER:	TITLE:	ADDRESS:
13.1.	Estil	The Farmer's Curst Wife VY	
13.2	Estil, Orna & Blair	The Cabin on the Hill XX (Orna voc & accordion Blair -voc)	

-cont-

TAPE:	PERFORMER:	TITLE:	ADDRESS:	TIME:
13.3.	Estil voc;guit Orna -voc. Blair -guit.	Jenny Jenkins XXYX (aka Ball)		2.35
13.4.	"	Take 2 OK		2.25
13.5.	Estil Voc-guit; Orna -voc. Blair -voc. Lacey -voc;guit.	Lonesome Valley XYYY		
13.6.	Estil	Wayfaring Stranger YXXXX (own arr.)		
13.7.	Estil	Father, Adieu. YXXX (own comp.)		

T-957

Chilhowie, Virginia. Sept. 3rd, 1952.

TAPE:	PERFORMER:	TITLE:	ADDRESS:	TIME:
14.0.	Horton Barker	A Rich Irish Lady Chilhowie, Va.		
14.1.	"	Three Nights Drunk		
14.2.	Spence Spencer Moore guit & voc Roy Everett Birns guit.	Jimmy Sutton XXX Route 2, Chilhowie,Va. Route 2, Chilhowie,Va.		
14.3.	"	Take 2 OK good new song		
14.4.	"	The Lawson Murder X (Birns-mandolin) arr. Spence		
14.5.	"	The Girl I Left Behind X		
14.6.	Spence Moore	Sixteen Tons Parody (comp. Spence)		
14.7.	Herd Time and	Hard Times a-Coming, (false start)		

T-958

Williamson, West Va. September 3rd, 1959.

TAPE:	PERFORMER:	TITLE:	ADDRESS:	TIME:
15.1.	Negro Extra Gang..... leader...Willie.	Dogging SteelXX -heavy		
15.2.	Fred McDowell...... with wife	Jesus Gonna Make Up\ My Dying Bed. XXX	Como, Miss.	

-cont-..

St. James Church, Howard St.

Huntsville, Ala. Baptism

No.	Title
15.3.	Long Meter Hymn... Lay Down, You Weary One, Lay Down. (good sound but distorted recording.)
15.4.	Prayer... poor, but good preaching.
15.5.	Baptism Invocation – ~~ordinary~~ rather ordinary preaching but remarkable responses. Very long. Gets better as candidate goes into the pool. Begins half way thru reel.
15.6.	Old Ship of Zion ... poor.
15.7.	I'll Meet You on Canaan's shore. (preacher and congregation.)

Mt. Olivet — T-859

The Regular Baptist Church, Blackey, Lecher County, Kentucky. Sept 5, 1959.

No.	Title
16.1.	Guide Me, Oh Thou Great Jehovah.(464) Led by Ike Caudill. XXXXX
16.2.	Heaven is Mine. The Pentecostal Temple at Memphis.

The Mount Olivet Regular Baptist Church, Blackey, Ky. Sept. 6th.

Ex

No.	Performer	Title
17.1.	Mrs & Mr Elmer Dickson.........	Come With Me to the Old Churchyard(28)
17.2.	Leader: E.D. Beck	When Jesus Christ Was Here Below.(74)
17.3.	"	Sweet Rivers of Redeeming Love.
17.4.	Preacher: D. N. Asher, Lecher, Lecher, Ky.	"Willing Soldiers for the Lord" is his theme.

NB: The numbers refer to the hymn number in "The New Baptist Song Book" revised and edited. Published: J. Ratcliff, Lookout, Ky.

T-861

The Mount Olivet Regular Baptist Church, Blackey, Ky. Sept.6th, 1959.

No.	Performer	Title
18.1.	Led: Jack Brownland	The Day is Past & Gone
18.2.	D.N. Asher.	Prayer
18.3.	I.D. Beck	Preaching
1814.	I.D. Beck	Poor Pilgrim of Sorrow XX (solo. Own tune)
18.5.	I.D. Beck	Preaching.
18.6.	Agan Back.lead.	Salvation, Oh the Name I Love.

T-861

Blackey, Ky. -cont-

No.	Performer	Title
19.1.	Agan Back.	Salvation, Oh the Name I love X X X –cont from tape 18.)
19.2.	I.D. Beck.	His last prayer.

Senatobia, Miss. September 26th, 1959.

No.	Performer	Title
19.3.	Mrs Sidney (Hemphill) Carter.	Worried Blues... Now Senatobia, Miss.
19.4.	"	Pharoah X X X X X
19.5.	"	Leather Britches
19.6.	Ruby Stein Hemphill Bobby Jean Hemphill Lucille Rice	Pease Porridge
19.6.	" " "	Little Sally Walker (3 times)
19.7.	" " "	In and Out the Window, Cindy.
19.8. S	Sydney Carter	Leave Nobody But the Baby
19.9.	" "	Everybody Oughta Treat a Stranger Right
19.10.	Three girls	Cornbread Rough, Cornbread Tough.
19.11.	" "	Hold Up the Gatepost
19.12.	" "	Jumpety Jump
19.13.	" "	BumbleBee Done Stang Me
19.14.	" "	Sally Go Round the Sunshine
19.15.	" "	Red Bird

TAPE:	PERFORMER: T-863	TITLE:	ADDRESS:
The Thornton Regular Baptist Church, Mayking, Ky. Sept. 7, 1959.			
Leader:			
20.1.	George Spangler	Brethren, We've Met Again XX	Mayking, Ky.
20.2.	" " "	Guide Me, Oh Thou Great Jehovah	
20.3.	Howard Adams	One Night While the Moon Was Shining From Heaven	Whitesburg, Ky.
20.4.	" " "	Amazing Grace	
20.5.	" " "	And Must This Body Die ?	
20.6.	Raymond Collins	Oh Ye Young, Ye Gay.	Whitesburg, Ky.

T-864

The Thornton Regular Baptist Church - II

21.

- - - - - - - - - - - - - - - - - - -
T-865
Ada Combs, Whitesburg, Ky. Tape 22.

A transcription from the Miniature recorder. She tells about hunting, snake-handlers, boa-constrictors and hippo she saw, banjo tunes, accidents, killings.

- - - - - - - - - - - - - - - - - - -
T-866
Ada Combs, Whitesburg, Ky. Tape 23.

Her tunes; corn-shucking, fights, wives and husbands.
- - - - - - - - - - - - - - - - - - -

TAPE:	PERFORMER:	TITLE:	ADDRESS:
T-867			
24.1.	George Fields, fiddle	Nigger and a White Man Playing 7 Up	Lexington, Ala.
24.2.	"	Bob Johnson's Tune	
24.3.	"	Pie Crust	
24.4.	"	Billy In the Low Grounds (or Madagascar)	
24.5.	"	Stoney Point (Civil War)	
24.6.	"	The Pat and Mike Story.	

NB: The first thing on the tape is conversation between George Fields and Lonnie Odum.

T-868

25.1.	Albert Hammond Emma Hammond fiddle –banjo	8th of January	Lexington, Ala.
25rt:			
25.2.	"	Haste to the Wedding	
25.3.	Emma Hammond	Laura Lee–banjo & song	
25.4.	"	Catfish ("")	
25.5.	"	Dewdrop Waltz –played twice (banjo solo) comp. her brother	
26.6.	"	Jaybird (")	
25.7.	Cleveland Hurts	Live and Let Live (Guitar & harmonica)	Rte 2, Lexington,
25.8.	Emma & Albert	The Rabbit Dance –from his nephew 25 yrs ago (Emma banjo)Albert dancing) at Brush Creek,nr. (Tune:Knock John Booker) Florence, Alabama.	
25.9.	Emma	Wiley Chords I (from brother) solo	
25.10.	"	Wiley Chords II –(Dewdrop Waltz) "	
25.11.	"	The F-Chord Tune (Very lovely)	
25.12.	"	Camp Meeting (twice)	
25.13.	"	Joree's Scratch (from William Riley) (twice)	
25.14.	"	Alabama Girls	

TAPE:	PERFORMER:	TITLE:	ADDRESS:
25.15.	Emma Hammond	No Name Scratch. ("Kindly like Hen Cackle.")	
25.16.	"	Jenny Lind Polka	
25.17.	"	Emma's Delight (same as No Name Scratch)	
25.18.	"	Great Big Yam Potato.	
25.19.	"	Indian Pudding & Pumpkin Pie.	

NB: THE RABBIT DANCE Bent over with hand, not knees, on floor. Two pats on back of hand; turn palm and slap on floor; two pats back of other hand; turn palm, slap on floor, etc. End: Two beats left hand, 3 right hand.

T-869

Tape 26: Sacred Harp Convention at Fyffe, Ala, Sept. 12, 1959.

TAPE:	PERFORMER:	TITLE:	ADDRESS:
26.1.		Aylesbury (28)	
26.2.	Dr. M.O Slaughter of Texas	Invitation (327)	
26.3.	"	Greenwich (183)	
26.4.	?	Columbiana (56) end only	
26.5.	Mr. Boyd	Cusseta (73)	
26.6.	"	Eostasy (106)	
26.7.	Mary Johnson	Morning Prayer (411)	
26.8.	"	Sabbath Morning(283)	
26.9.	M.W. Light	Logan (302)	
26.10	"	Melancholy Day (419)	
26.11.	Mary Wood 12 yr old.	Minister's Farewell (69)	
26.12.	"	The Child of Grace (77)	
26.13.	Max Golden	The Bower of Prayer (100)	
26.14.	"	The Church's Desolation (89)t tape ran out	

TAPE: T-870	PERFORMER:	TITLE:	ADDRESS:
	Sacred Harp — II		
27.1.	Laura Stricken	Victoria (290)	
27.2.		Protection (402)	
27.3.	Ray Hughes	Heavenly Rest (403)	
27.4.	"	Burk (92)	
27.5.	Sally Gallen	Sacred Mount (456)	
27.6.	"	Morgan (304)	
27.7.	Jim Ayres	Doddridge (263)	
27.8.	"	Hungtington (193)	
27.9.	?	Southwell (365)	
27.10	Jessie McCullers	The Fountain (397)	
27.11.	"	Delight (216)	

T-871			
	Sacred Harp — III		
28.1.	Hubert King	The Marcellas (405)	
28.2.	"	Hallelujah (146)	
28.3.		Business meeting;elections.	
28.4.	Bud McGraw	New Hope (316)	
28.5.	"	Burdette (422)	
28.6.	Mrs Leslie Crowden	Fellowship (330)	
28.7.	"	A Cross For Me (349) (349)	

After lunch:

28.8.	Started in middle .		
28.9.	same woman	Soar Away (455)	
28.10.	Mr. M. O.Kennedy	Eden (200)	
28.11.		Mount Zion (220)	
28.12.	Irene Parker	Arbacoochee (430)	
28.13.	"	Anthem of the Savior (355)	

Sacred Harp VII
T-175

	PERFORMER	TITLE	ADDRESS
32.1.	??	Present Joys (118)(frag.)	
32.2.	Mrs Tom Hight	Oxford (306) xxx	
32.3.	"	Fleeting Days (348) x	
32.4.	Eugene Dawson	Sherburne (186) xxxx	
32.5.	"	Northfield (155) xxxx	
32.6.	Valerie Jo McCullers	Eternal Home (336) x	
32.7.		Sardis (460) x	
32.8.	Bill Matthews	Baptismal Anthem (232)	
32.9.		Heavenly Vision (250) words only	
32.10.	Jim Ayres	Consecration (448)	
32.11.	A.L. Parker	Arbacoochee (430)	
32.12.		Notes Almost Divine (396)	
32.13.	Enis Nall	Crantville (423) xxxx - lively, a bit hard	
32.14.		Loving Jesus (361) xxx - lively, trival melody xxxx	
32.15.	Velma Johnson,Ga.	The Last Words of Copernicus (Atlanta, Ga.) (112) - lively, good parts	
32.16.		Victoria (290) xxx-slow-hard- powerful gd parts - pero me again	

Distinctive →

T-174
Sacred Harp VIII

33.1.	W.V. Kidd	Antioch (277)-slow, lovely old tune xxxx	
33.2.	"	Windham (38) big, mournful, slow, beautiful. xxx	
33.3.	Mrs Maud Quinn	Sinners Friend (132) xxx	
33.4.		Travelling On (208) lively xxxxx	
33.5.	Laurie Denson	Masonic Ode (228) n.g.	
33.6.	Mrs King Roberts	Wondrous Love (159) words only. xxxxx	
33.7.	C.C. Matthews	Return Again (335) xx	
33.8.		Homeward Bound (373) xxxx lively, good parts	
33.9	Virginia Dell Shrader	Amsterdam (84)	

33.10.	Virginia Dell Shrader	The Grieved Soul (448) x	
33.11.	John Alexander	Soldier of the Cross (325)	
33.12.	"	Manchester (392) good, lively xxx	
33.13.	B.F. Ship	Mount Pleasant (218) xxx	

T-177
Sacred Harp IX

34.1.	B.F. Ship	Norwich (362)	
34.2.	Homer Murphy	Claremount (245) v.long	
34.3.	J.W. Ashley	Westford (280)	
34.4.		North Port (324)	
34.5.	Bob Leith	Providence (298)	
34.6.	Mrs Woody Walker	Adoration (138)	
34.7.	Martin Blackmon	Cusseta (73) (words only for memorial)	
34.8.		New Britain (45) (***)	
34.9.	Special group	Weeping Mary (408)	
34.10.	"	Christmas Anthem (225)	
34.11.	"	Invocation (131) (words only)	

T-178
Sacred Harp X

35.1.	Special Gp	New Prospect (390) words only xx	
35.2.	"	David's Lamentation (268) (words only)	
35.3.	J.H. Lambert	Montgomery (189)	
35.4.	"	Invitation (327)	
35.5.	Mrs Botts	Weeping Sinners (108)	
35.6.	"	Confidence (270)	

--cont.--

T-879

TAPE:	PERFORMER:	TITLE:	ADDRESS:
35.7.	J. Edge	Canaan's Land (101)	
35.8.	"	The Morning Trumpet (85)	
35.9.	Uncle Will Larrin=k	Melancholy (419)	
35.10.	"	Protection (402)	
35.11.	Mrs Allen	The Church's Desolation (89)	
35.12.	"	I Would See Jesus (75) x-x	good quality
35.13.	Otis Parker	Louisiana (207) x x	" "
35.14.	"	Ragan (176) - Farewell Vain World - xxxx strong legume	
35.15.	Sylvia Wooton	Blooming Youth (176) x x x	
35.16.	"	Calvary (300) - exc. xxx xxx	
35.17.	J.W. Webb	Praise God (328) - exc. x x lively, rich, well-length	
35.18.	J. H. Carter	Symphony (151) - fiddly - good quality - paste, unplay	

T-879

Sacred Harp — II

TAPE:	PERFORMER:	TITLE:	ADDRESS:
36.1.	J.H. Carter	Fredericksburg (389)	
36.2.	Mr. Wilburn	The Promised Land (128)-exc.	
36.3.	"	New Jordan (442) - exc	
36.4.	Foy Frederick	Christ Our Song (386)	
36.5.	"	New Bethel (395)	
36.6.	Arlan Webb	Logan (302)	
36.7.	"	Morgan (304) (words only)	
36.8.	Lloyd Redding	Easter Anthem (236) (words only)	
36.9.	C.H. Galloway	Odem (340$)	
36.10.	"	Lena (210)	
36.11.	Joyce Smith	She talks first Send a Blessing (369) (disturbed)	

T-880

TAPE:	PREACHER:	TITLE:	ADDRESS:
	Sacred Harp XII	This tape is moving on one track	
37.1.	Joyce Smith	Funeral Anthem (320)	
37.2.		Business - very good...	
37.3.	Mr. Holly	Bear Creek (269) --unuseable	
37.4.	"	Hilford (272)	
37.5.	Bob Teifel	Mount Zion (220)	
37.6.	"	Bishop (420)	
37.7.	Lee Phillips	The Better Land (454)	
37.8.	"	The Marriage in the Skies (438)	
37.9.	Lonnie West	New Prospects (390) not complete.	

T-881

Sacred Harp XIII

Tape 38:

38.1. Long Meter Hymn from Thornton Regular Baptist Chuch, Mayking, Ky.

Sacred Harp XIII

TAPE:	PREACHER:	TITLE:	ADDRESS:
38.2.	Lonnie West	New Prospect (390) (words only)	
38.3.	Dr. Slaughter	Arkansas (271) (level varies - jumping)	
38.4.	R.D. Lassiter	Never Turn Back (378) (bad wow)	
38.5.	"	Family Bible (165)	
38.6.		The closing prayer, goodbyes and speeches as they prepare to leave.	
	and	Amazing Grace........	
		no - We'll All Sing Hallelujah.	
		final prayer, in Methodist weeping style...	

TAPE: T-984   PERFORMER: TITLE: ADDRESS: T

Parchman, Miss, Camp 11, September 18th, 1959.

39.1. Floyd Batts (ldr) Dollar Mamie XX   3008 Marion Dunbar, Jackson.
    (3 or 4 men)
39.2. L.C. Hoskins   Tom Devil XXX   Drew, Miss.
39.3. Ernest Woodson   Rosie) (Slow, Stereo-quiet harmony)
                          Tom Devil (solo)
39.4. ~Floyd Batts/Woodson Dato Lucky Song (holler) X
39.5. ~Ernest Woodson   Dangerous Blues (holler) XX

T-983
Parchman, Miss, Camp 7.
leader:
40.1. Leroy Miller   Berta, Berta:... .....Tupelo, Miss.
                          (large gp. hoeing)
40.2. Clifton Haughton Going to Memphis (") short ng Amory, Miss.
40.3. Grover Wells   Rosie-Rosie (")X   Starksville, Miss.
40.4. Clyde Jones   Lazarus (") ng
40.5. Grover Wells   John Henry (") short; poor.
40.6. Leroy Gary   Momma Lucy -holler xx-dizzy
40.7. Henry Ratcliff   Look for me in Louisiana   Clarksdale, Miss.
                          (wonderful lonely voice) X X X
40.8. Leroy Grant   Forty Miles XX   Jackson, Miss.
                          (wonderful voice)
40.9. Grover Wells   Moaning Song X X
                          (Tender, sweet)
40.10. "   Little Baby X
40.11. Bugger Wells   Little Frenchman ....Eupora, Miss.
    L.K. Bedford
40.12. Clifton Haughton Captain George   —Columbus, Miss
    Leroy Grant
    Walter Hood

TAPE: PERFORMER: TITLE: ADDRESS:

Parchman, Miss, Camp 7.

41.1. Leroy Miller   Alberta XX (stereo farm)   Gulfport, Miss.
    Grover Wells   (ref: Oo-sa) axe ....
    Albert Coulbertson.
    Leroy Grant
    Walter Hood
41.2. Jerry Kennedy   Berta Say She Love Me
    (2817)   (4 men on axes)
41.3. "   Boats Up the River (") X
41.4. "   Captain George (") XXX
                          (good rhythm & singing)
41.5. James Campbell   Stewball (hoe) XX (good stereo)
    & several leaders   Int. text, good rhythm, singing)

Groups as follows:

41.2. Jerry Kennedy...2718 Swift St, Jackson. 23.
    J.D. Thomas....3333 Rigman Ave, Jackson. 18
    Dunhill Wright..845 Gloucester St, Greenville.
    Ernest Jones...158 Hall St, Houston, Miss.
41.3. James Campbell...(42)(7½-1st) Swiftown, Miss. Box 104,
    Ernest Woodson...2006 10th (or 70th ?) Ave, Meridian, (1st)
    John Oliver Evans, c/o Rosalie Butler, 224 West Washburn St. Clarksdal
    L.C. Hoskins....21644 Parchman. (6 more mths) Drew, Miss.
41.4. Same as 3, with Ernest Woodson, lead.
41.5. James Campbell leader, then:
    Fred Paine, 981 North Broadway, Greenville.

T-985
Tape 42: Miss. Pen. Lambert. Camp B.
leader:
42.1. John Edwards   Berta X
                          axes, good stereo, put on leader;
                          katydids, not good tune, good wk song   1int)
42.2. George Golden   Stewball-axes XX X
42.3. Ed Lewis   Black Gal XXXX
                          ('turns into Berta)-axes
42.4. George Golden   Berta (good text & leader) XX X X
                          (turns into Berta)-axes
42.5. Ed Lewis   John Henry (train pass,)-axes X X
42.6. Ed Lewis   Stewball -hoes, XXX (qd stereo)
N.B. This one recorded with line moving past the three mikes.
42.7. George Golden   Po' Lazarus. XX X 2

Turn page over
for address

Personnel for Tape 42.

Ed Lewis (17½ years on farm) 36yrs. Sister -- 1926 Clara Ave, St, Louis 12, Mo (# 14328)

George Golden (9yrs 3mths). 9 mths more. 1003 Maple St, Jackson, Miss. (# 25129)

John Edmonds 47yrs old, (5 yrs. 9 yrs to go.) 3818 Deer St, Chicago, Ill. Farm-band from Darling, Miss.)

Willie P. Robertson. 8036 P O Ensley, Ala. # 22121

Wesley Lee Brown # 21252 Woodlawn, 316, W. Moore, Greenville.

Henry Mason, 22078; Rte 1, Box 3-69, Bolton, Miss.

Oscar Crosby 23863; Rte 1, Box 29, Marks, Miss.

Robert Lewis, 25605; 601 Felicity, New Orleans.

James Carter, 24648.

Heuston Barnes -13319.

Johnny Moore 21263.

Willie Matthews 19750 (or 6)

TAPE:	PERFORMER:	TITLE:	ADDRESS:
Miss. Pen. Lambert Camp B.			
43.1.	Ed Lewis	I Be So Glad When the Sun Goes Down -- hossblg gd. gd. stereo. xxxx	
43.2.	Lee Johnny/Moore (21263)	Eighteen Hammers - ("")xxxx	351 S. Harvey St., Greenville.
43.3.	Johnny Moore	Levee Holler (Money-waster break)	
43.4.	Ed Lewis	Levee Holler xx	
43.5.	James Carter	Po' Lazarus(big gd.) plus xxx interview about Lazarus. Wind noise.)	

T-867
Lambert Camp B.

44.1.	Ed Lewis John L. Moore James Carter & Henry Mason	Dollar Mamie xxx (good stereo) (with 3 men. axxx; gd text)	
44.2.	Ed Lewis etc.	Too Devil, ("")Raise axes on "Oh Yeah" xxx½ (good stereo)	

T-868
Lambert Camp B:

45.1.		Interview with Ed Lewis about work songs, etc.	
45.2.	Ed Lewis	John Henry-solo	
45.3.	Heuston Barnes -	Rosie - Style A	Heuston aged 43. 11 year: in pen; since mother died no home address, No.13319.
45.4.	"	" Style B	
45.5.	"	" Style C.	

T-869
Lambert Camp B.

46.1.	Heuston Barnes ...	Ain't Been Able to Get Back Home No Mo'. Axe sor xx	
46.2.	"	Starboll - axe song.	
46.2.A.		Statement about work songs, and prison experience. xxxx	
46.3.		I Been Havin' Troubles (fs. st) -holler XX Composed on the spot.	
46.4.		Interview. xxx	

TAPE: T-890	PERFORMER:	TITLE:	ADDRESS:

Lambert Camp B.

47.1. Houston Barnes — Stewball / with eleven men, hoes. / well sung; a broken warrant.

47.2. Johnny Lee Moore — Early in the Morning ××××

47.3. Fragments - cancel

NB: Then: Free Springs Church; Panola County, Miss.

47.4. Girls' Choir — Runnin' For Jesus ××

47.5. Boy's Choir — Lord, I Tried - cancel

47.6. Viola James — I'm Going Home to live with Jesus ×××× / (one chorus needs cutting)

47.7. Young girl — Then Melinda Sings / (Poet Laurence)

47.8. Young man — Let My Last Day Be My Best

47.9. On My 'Pointed Time — Yg man

47.10. I'm Gonna Wait Till My Change Shall Come (are these last 2 1 son.

47.11. Church — Soon One Morning. / 'Beginning defective; good patches, / shd get better.)

- - - - - - - - -

T-84j
Free Springs Church, Panola County.

48.1. Ed Young -fife / Viola James, Rte 1, Box 92 / Como, Miss. / Lonnie Young Sr -drum / Lonnie Young Jr -drum / Patting group — O Let Me Ride ××× (Cong. Free Springs Meth Ch.) / Slow-gaited, good (Harmonsville, Penola Co.) / cong.

- - - - - - - - -

T-84j

49.1. Ed Young -fife / Lonnie Young Sr -drum / Lonnie Young Jr -drum / Patting group — 1463 Dunn St,Apt 30f / Rte 1, Como. Memphis. / Rte 1, Como.

49.2. all — Oree (twice) ×× / ×××

Jim and John ×××× [This not used on At / (Lonnie Sr. vocal,) / interview with Shirley ending in laughter.

49.3. all — Sitting On Top of the World ×××× / (Lonnie - vocal)

49.4. all — Chevrolet -Lonnie voc. ×××× / Best stereo so far.

-cont.-

TAPE:	PERFORMER:	TIME:	ADDRESS:

#OOM=49

49.5. Lonnie and gp — Oree ××××× [This is cut actually / Atlantic record.

49.6. " — Jim and John ××××× / (very good start)

49.7. group — On That Rock ××××× / (group vocal) (for spectrachum)

NB: The patters are: Viola James, Route 1, Box 92, Como, Miss. / Elisha Franklinn, Rte 1, Box 119,Como / William Major James, Rte 1, Box 92 . Viola's son.

Monday 21st Sept: T-84j

50.1. Ed Young / Lonnie Jr & Sr. — Church, I Know We Got ×× / Another Building. (v.g. start / (Lovely tune- use sp. recd.)

50.2. " — Jim and John (no vocal) ××× / (Fine sound)

50.3. everyone — Hen Duck (Lonnie vocal) claps; ××××× / Afrikan; lovely sound) v. old tune.

22nd Sept.

50.4. Fred McDowell -guit — Shake 'Em On Down ×××× Rte 1, Como. / Danny Davis -comb -sist (stereo) Box 109.0omo / Miles Pratcher-guit Rte 1, Como.

50.5. same gp. — "I'm Going Down To the River ×××××× / (stereo)

50.6. " — Take 2. Diff; mixing.better.

50.7. Miles Pratcher -guit. — It's All Night Long ××× / Bob Pratcher -fiddle. Miles vocal. Words clear. / Fine stereo.

50.8. 'same — Joe Turner. / crude- interesting historically.

oooooooooooooooooo

(Right section)

TAPE:	PERFORMER:	TITLE:	ADDRESS:
52.8.	Sid Hemphill quills Lucius Smith banjo	Emmeline, Take Your Time XX	Senatobia, Miss. Rte 1, Box 110 (Mattie Reed, daugh in)
52.9.	"	Walking in the Parlow and talk XX	
52.9,52.10.	"	Banjo and drums together no title	
52.10.	Lucius Smith	Make Tulu Behave XXX —banjo solo—cross noted tuning	
52.11.	"	Memphis Blues —banjo solo—single noted tuning (Handy? Written by Sid Hemphill if I know it ?"	
52.12.	"	Goodbye Honey, You Call That Gone XXX	
52.13.	Sid Hemphill	Hey Polly, Will You Marry Me (song and banjo both sid.) exc. tune)	
52.14.	"	The Banjo Man	

T-894

TAPE:	PERFORMER:	TITLE:	ADDRESS:
53.1.	Sid Hemphill	The Banjo Man (song and banjo) and interview XX	
53.2.	"	Don't Let My Rabbit Get Away X (no banjo)	
53.2.A.	Sid & Lucius	Same, but Lucius plays banjo	
53.3.	Sid Hemphill	Beaver Dam —song X	
53.4.	Sid & Lucius	Come on Boys, Let's Go the the Bell (quills and drums) XXX	
53.5.	Sid & Lucius	The Old Devil's Dream XXX (Sid quills & vocal, Lucius Drums)	
53.6.	"	Old Blues (violin & banjo) HISTORY !!	
53.7.	"	Blues (violin & banjo) HISTORY !!	

Independence Church, Tyro, Miss.

TAPE:	PERFORMER:	TITLE:	ADDRESS:
53.8.	Anderson Burton	God's Unchanging Hand XXX	Rte 2, Box 144, Cool Water, Miss.
53.9.	Viola James	Tyin' to Make Heaven My Home XXXX	1.30
53.10.	Velma Lucas	Rocka My Soul in the Bosom of Abraham.	Rte 5, Box 119, Hollow Springs.

* applause at end of these last three.

TAPE:	PERFORMER:	TITLE:	ADDRESS:
Monday Sept. 21st, 1959.			
51.1.	Miles & Bob Pratcher	If It's All Night Long, XXXX Baby, Take Your Time (album-lovely)	
51.2.	"	Joe Turner, XXX (poor, readg. intrstg for book)	
51.3.	"	Buttermilk XXXXX (good text, Rag & blues - sn, dance)	
51.4.	"	Bill Bailey X (words OK)	
51.5.	"	Old Hen Cackle, Run Get the Egg XX (very crude)	
51.6.	"	I'm Gonna Anyhow Till I Die XXX (good new song)	
51.7.	Fred McDowell, Miss Pratcher	When You Get Home Please Write Me a Few of Your Lines. XXXX	
51.8.	"	Drop Down Mama, X XXX	
51.9.	"	Blues, XXXXX — I'm going down south— big medium tempo with comb solo struct.	
51.10.	"	Shake 'Em on Down XXX (stereo not m.terif,rhythm)	

T-895

TAPE:	PERFORMER:	TITLE:	ADDRESS:
52.1.	Mattie Gardener, Ida Mae Towns, Jessie Lee Pratcher	I'm Bound to Get to XXX Heaven at Last (for special album)	Rte 1, Box 170,Como. Rte 1, Box 185,Como. Rte 1, Como.
52.2.	same gp.	Green Sally Up XXXX	1.00
52.3.	"	Little Sally Walker XX	
52.4.	Jessie L. Pratcher	Mary Mack	.40
52.5.	"	Take 2 - XXX	.3
52.6.	Little Gardner	Mary Mack (lovely new text)	1.40
52.7.	Denise Gardner, Mattie Gardner, Ida Mae Towns, Lucille Powell	I Wish I Was in Heaven XXX Sitting Down. (melody)	
52.8. —cont—			

T-847

Tape	Performer	Title	Address	Time
53.1.	Louise Green	I'm a Soldier In The Army of the Lord ✗✗	Rte 1, como.	.5
54.2.	Mary Lee (wife of Rev)	Jesus Is Real To Me✗✗✗✗	Rte 1,Box 137, Senatobia.	3.0
54.3.	Evelina McClathery	Certainly Lord ✗	Rte 5,Box 135 Holly Springs.	3.1
54.4.	James Shorty	This Little Light of Mine (and Need B Work)✗✗✗✗	Box 11,Rte 2, Senatobia.	2,3
54.5.	Viola James	Is There Anybody Here That Loves My Jesus.✗✗✗		2.5
54.6.	James Shorty	Jesus On the Main Line ✗✗ (end by Viola James)		3.3
54.7.	The Independent Choir.H.C. Lee at piano & voo.lead. Son of Rev. Lee	I'm Pressing On (organiser.Louise Green)		
54.7.	The Choir	O Mary Doncha Weep Viola James, lead.		
54.8.	Fred McDowell	Worried Life Blues ✗✗✗		3.20
54.9.	"	61 Highway Blues —perfect. ✗✗✗✗✗✗		3.10

54.10.— T-847

September 25th, 1959, Penola Co.

Tape	Performer	Title	Address	Time
55.1.	Felix Dukes -voo McDowell -guit.	Motherless Children ✗✗✗✗	Rt 2,Bx 82,Como.	2.45
55.2.	Fred McDowell voo - and guit.	Lord, Have Mercy (trug)		1.10
55.3.	Fred -voo & guit	You Done Told Everybody In ✗✗✗✗ Your Neighborhood. -terif,guit.		5.00
55.4.	Longtown Pilgrim Travelers	Move Up ✗	Ed McNeill .Rt 2, Bx 82, Como.	2.15
55.5.	Fred McDowell	I Woke Up This Morning		3.10
55.6.	"	Soon One Morning ✗✗✗✗		3.05
55.7.	"	Keep Yr Lamps Trimmed & Burning✗✗✗✗✗		2.40
55.8.	"	Wisht I Was in Heaven Sitting Down bad ending ✗✗✗		2.05
55.9.	"	" same, but faster.		

NB: Talented dancer-singer - Raymond Walker, Rt 2, Box 202, Como. 26 yrs. and Ethel Wilbur, exc. dancer.

T-847

Tape	Performer	Title	Address	Time
56.1.	Sidney and Rose Hemphill(sistrs)	When The Train ✗✗✗ Come Along (Fred,guitar) ✗✗	Senatobia, Miss.	
56.2.	Rose with guit (Roselie Hill)	Rolled & Tumbled Blues ✗✗✗✗		2.50
56.3.	Fred McDowell	Germany Blues ✗✗✗✗	Rte 1, Box 204A, Como.	3.50
56.4.	"	Good Morning, Little School.girl✗✗✗✗✗		2:50
56.5.	Fred&guit & voo Fanny Davis -cor-b Miles Pratcher-guit	Goin' Down to the River ✗✗✗✗ (gd stereo.)		7.45
56.6.	Lonnie Young-fife Lonnie Jr -tin can	Oree		
56.7.	Fred McDowell	Freight Train Blues ✗✗✗✗		
56.8.	Roselie Hill	Bullying Well ✗✗✗		
56.9.	James Shorty Fred-guit.	Mother Died & Left Me ✗✗✗ (own comp.)		
56.10.	ditto	I Want Jesus to Walk With Me (Best first part to be joined on)		

T-906

Tape	Performer	Title	Address	Time
57.1.	James Shorty Fred -guit	I Want Jesus To Walk With Me ✗✗✗✗✗ Three takes. 3rd good.		
57.2.	Roselie Hill	Faro - good text		
57.3.	Mr & Mrs McDowl	Keep Yr Lamps Trimmed & Burning (pretty but doesn't work)		
57.4.	Fred McDowell ✗✗✗✗ (lovely-noisy-needs work)			
57.5.	"	Worried Life Blues ✗✗		
57.6.	"	I Been Drinkin' Water Out of a ✗✗✗✗✗ Hollow log. (very old blues - extra fine reedg.)		

TAPE: PERFORMER: TITLE: ADDRESS:

T-901

Quartets at St. Peter Church, Tate Co. Miss. Sept. 1959. Save as document

St. Louis Quartet:

58.1. Have You Ever Heard a Man Speak Like This Before ? -frag. X (fantastic sound effect.)

58.2. The Old Ship of Zion

58.3. Got On my Travelin' Shoes (very hot and harsh frag)XXX

Detroit Quartett

58.4. Intro - very funny, jazzy, leader Willie Ayres, Bros Jones, Owens, McGhee.

58.5. Trees - mad !! and very long. Lead too far in b.g.

58.6. No One Else Than Him - The Lockhart Temple, Memphis.

T-902

The Hart Temple, Memphis, Pastor Lockhart (Bishop) Oct.3rd, 1959.

Rev. L.L. Lockhart 303 South 3rd, Memphis. S. Garner soloist & guit, 280 Hernando.

59.1. Lockhart's Opening Prayer

59.2. The Congregation - Sing To The Power of the Lord (harsh, jumpy, ugly.)

59.3. Radio commercials - then Robert Sim, Marion, Ark, lead cong with I Know a Man. (guit. too heavy) X

59.4. Make it Somehow - cong. X

59.5. Testimony - n.g.

59.6. Praise - sung b Rev. Lockhart - poor

59.7. Sermon - Rev. Lockhart - frag. -fair X

59.8. That He Done For Me - Rev 1 and cong.

59.9. Hot Music on Guitra and Cymbals

59.10. Sing Till T e Power of the Lord Come Down (good example of Holy Roller singing, mod. electric guitar.) XXX

59.11. God is a Wonder - S. Garner solo. (typical gospel solo. Not bad.)

This service was held only for the broadcast, and when they went off the air everyone went home.....

TAPE: PERFORMER: TITLE: ADDRESS:

New Browns Chapel, Temporary Home of Greater Harvest M.B. Church.
Rev R.C. Crenshaw, pastor. XX

60.1. Rev. Crenshaw makes collection address - wonderful responces and lining hymn. He exhibits his harsh, howling style of moaning - some good spots.

60.2. I'm Going Home on the Morning Train - led Crenshaw. Good stereo. hard, rough and thrilling in a way.

60.3. Rev. Reynolds preaching - he's a Chicago man who told me he hates the old time emotional style. Last 3 mins are pretty good These: Paul in Philippi pr'son. "I Don't care what you say, singin Zion's songs will disturb heaven."

T-904

New Browns Chapel -II. Sunday 4th October, 1959. The Broadcast.

61.2. Dancha Know It'll Be Alright - gospel song, then announts by young woman, full credits, very unappealing.

61.2. Radio prayer with organ and piano b.g. Choir also fills. Useable.

61.3. Till The Power of the Lord Comes Down - choir, piano, organ, leader off mike

61.4. Did You Ever See a Man Like Jesus X - good ex, of hot gospel.

61.5. Vacation in Heaven - solo with piano and responses. Amusing as example of old spiritual type in gospel style.

61.6. Prayer.

61.7. Gospel song by choir. X

T-905

New Browns Chapel - 111

62.1. Get Right Church, And Let's Go Home - Rev C, choir, piano, organ. X

62.2. Sermon -Forgetting the Past - Rev C. I Love the Lord, he Hears XX
Mr Crm - Rev C and cong....."and pities every groan".."Long as I live where trouble rise. I hasten to God's throne." Then goes on to preach with choir moaning sweetly behind. In 3 minutes he is breathing like an animal. A sexual sound ?? The sermon takes 10 mins - is about Lot's Wife.

62.3. Free at Last, performed by Rev C, choir and cong.

62.4. Invitation to Church

62.5. Long Retro Hymn XX

Brown Chapel IV

63.1. Collection speech. Lining Hymn.
63.2. After service special sp: Steal Away. Good b.g. leader OK X X
63.3. I Couldn't Hear Nobody Pray - Crenshaw lead X X X
63.4. The Whole World In His Hands.

The Pentecostal Temple, Memphis, Tenn. Sunday Oct 4th, evening.

63.5. Prayer. n.g.
63.6. We Need Rain X
63.7. Testimony
63.8. Look Where He Brought Me From - male lead, cong and organ X X X
63.9. Nothing.
63.10. Jesus Keep (frag.
63.11. Collection ...bad..
63.12. Help Me Jesus - rhythm.

T-907

The Pentecostal Temple, Memphis, Tenn. Oct 4th. Bishop J.O. Patterson

64.1. Hymn - marvellous sound effects hard to unde-stand words.
64.2. Bishop Patterson begins sermon:v. cultivated; gd part third thru ends by singing "Yes."
A 64.3. That You Think About Jesus - pentecostal folk song. Gd begin but side boogy- Ted Dennis McLellan.
A 64.4. Power- foll: go g pentecostal. Madame Mattie Wigley. nosly by use
64.5. Rain Song - orig. Elder James Rogers.
64.6. Heaven is Mine - trad. - Mattie Wigley

T-908
65.1. Cecil Augusta(39)   Stop All the Boses X   Rte 1, Williston,
    (derived:Sonny Boy   Tenn.Sept 30, '59.
    Williamson)(Wd Sores)
65.2.   "   Crawford's Jump (self comp.)

--tape-cont--

Memphis Jug Band

TAPE	PERFORMER	TITLE	ADDRESS	TIME
65.3.	Charlie Burse -voc. Plus sp.	Kokomo X X X	639 Hernando Place Jackson 5-2210	2.55
65.4.	Charlie Burse -voc	Kokomo -2 n.g.		2.55
65.5.	"	West Indian Blues		2.30
65.6.	Will Shade & sp Burse-guit-Carter Corley bass Whit kazoo	I'm Going to Newport News	225 4th St. JA-74750	2.25
65.7.	Shade voc sp	Bet I'll Get a Break X X X		2.35

Personnel:Charlie Burse, voc & guit; Robert Carter, elec.guit.
1456 Southern Ave, Memphis; Dewey Corley, jug and bass and kazoo,
197 South 4th, Apt.1. JA 75604; Will Shade, voc, bass and washboard,
Whiskey - Eugene Smith - 321½ Beale St.

T-909
Hughes, Ark. October 1st, 1959.

TAPE	PERFORMER	TITLE	ADDRESS	TIME
66.0.	Forrest City Joe	Blues Before Sunrise	Joe B.Pugh Gen.Deliv,Hughes.	
66.1.	F.C. Joe	Drink On Little Girl (with steel guitars)		
65.2.		You Gotta Cut That Out (")		
66.3.	F.C. Joe Sonny Boy Rogers guit. Thomas Martin-drums	She Lived Her Life Too Fast X X X	Rte 1, Box 263 Hughes, Ark. Gen. Deliv, Hughes	3.0
A 66.4.	Forrest City Joe	She Don't Love Me Thataway		3.2
A 66.5.		Forrest City Jump		3.0
A 66.6.	Boy Blue Hayes (no contacts;all orig. songs) Willie Jones-guit	Boogie Children X X X X	Roland Hayes Hughes, c/o E.J.Chatman,Tu.	2.44
A 66.7.	Boy Blue	Boy Blue Rock.		

extra address in box: Darnel Walker, Rte 1, Box 322, Hughes.

TAPE: Hughes –II   T-910

No.	PERFORMER	TITLE	ADDRESS	TIME
57.1.	Willie Jones & Boy Blue gp	You Got Dimples in Your Jaws XX		
A 67.2.	P.C. Joe & gp	Stop Breaking Down XX		2.4
67.3.	"	Forest City Boogie XXXX needs fading Drink On		3.0
A 67.4.	"			
A 67.5.	"	She lived Her Life Too Fast XXXX		3.10
67.6.	Willie Washington	Rocks Is My Pillow (own comp)	c/o Ollie Moore Hughes	
A 67.7.	Boy Blue	Joe Lee's Rock XXXXX		3.3
67.8.		Joe Lee's Rock –take 2 (beging cd be better)		2.4

Hughes –III   T-911

No.	PERFORMER	TITLE	ADDRESS	TIME
A 68.1.	P.C. Joe with harmonica	Down on the Levee Blues XXX		7.50
A 68.2.	"	Train Time XXXXXX (one break at 3.10)		6.00
A 68.3.	with piano	Red Cross Sto XXXX		4.25

T-912

No.	PERFORMER	TITLE	ADDRESS	TIME
69.1.	Elmeda Riddle	House Carpenter	Miller, Ark. Rt 3, Box 122 Hot Springs, Ark.	
69.2.	"	Family History		
69.3.	"	Jesse James (frag)		
59.4.	"	Golden Willow Tree (frag)		
A 69.5.	"	Froggie Went Courting (2 ends)		
69.6.	"	Bury Me Beneath the Willow.		

Timbo, Ark. October 6th.

No.	PERFORMER	TITLE	ADDRESS	TIME
69.7.	Neil Morris	Turnip Greens		
69.8.	"	The Juice of the Forbidden Fruit.		

TAPE: | **PERF NOS:** | **TITLE:** | **ADDRESS:** | **TIME:** 1.00

No.	PERF	TITLE	ADDRESS
A 70.1.	Neil Morris	Little Moses XX	Mountainview, Ark.
70.2.	"	Corn Rodgers X (Little Lee Hayes, wonderful words.) Interview abt song iverse abt preacher and Oscar's verse. Anything. X	
70.3.	....	....	
70.4.	"	Interview about family (matl for book. Extra good.)	
70.5.	"	The Lass of Loch Royal XXX	
70.6.	"	Willie Brennan "Ocar Gilbert's favorite song)	

T-913

No.	PERF	TITLE	ADDRESS
71.1.	Neil Morris	Soldier & the Lady	
71.2.	"	Interview about Jesse James	

T-914

No.	PERF	TITLE	ADDRESS
A 71.3.		Jesse James	
71.4.	Charlie Everidge mouth-bow Neil Morris caller	Turkey in the Straw	Mountainview, Ark.
71.5.	both	Sally Goodin	
A 71.6.		Wave the Ocean, Wave the Sea	
71.7.	Neil Morris	Down on the Banks of the Arkansas.	
71.8.		Rock All the Babies to Sleep (from Jimmie Rodgers record.)	

T-915

No.	PERF	TITLE	ADDRESS
72.1.	Mrs Ollie Gilbert	The Diver Boy XX, (Edmund in the lowlands)	Timbo, Ark.
72.2.	"	Once I Courted a Lady Beauty Bright (noisy)	
72.3.	"	Joseph Looney. X (local death-bed song)	
72.4.	"	It Rained a Mist XXX (The Jew's Garden)	
72.5.	"	Willow Green –fr X Y exc text. 1 verse missing	

–cont–

TAPE:	PERFORMER:	TITLE:	ADDRESS:
8"/72.6.	Oscar Gilbert	Go Preach Into the Wilderness -exolt (nigger problem)	Timbo, Ark.
72.7.	"	Cole Younger	
72.8. 72.8A	Ollie Gilbert	Sugar Hill -banjo solo / Soldier's Joy	
72.9.	Carlos Shannon ("Buckmiller")	Buffalo Gals	Timbo, Ark.
72.10.	"	8th of January	
72.11.	"	Cotton Eye Joe	
72.12	"	Down Arkansas Among the STICKS (from Major Vandyke-passing musician)	
72.13.	Ollie Gilbert	The Western Cowboy	
72.14.	"	Pretty Polly Oliver	
72.15.	"	Lord Bateman	
72.16.	"	The Little Family (mary, Martha & lazarus)	
72.17.	"	Who Will Shoe Your Foot ?	
T-916			
73.1.	Abey Morrison fiddler -63	Bonaparte's Charge	Landes, Ark.
73.2.	"	Bonaparte's Retreat	
73.3.	"	Cornwallis' March	
73.4.	"	Tip Toe Betty Martin	
73.5.	"	Sheep and Goats Gone to the Pasture "bow's a slippin' on that one pretty bad"	
73.6.	"	A Virginia Tune (march)	
73.7.	"	The Scotch Musick	
73.8.	"	Nancy's Got a Pretty Dress On	
73.9.	"	Prettiest Girl in Town (Va.)	

--cont-

TAPE:	PERFORMER:	TITLE:	
8"/73.10.	Abey Morrison	Alabama Girls	
73.11.	"	My Pretty Little Gal is Gone (About his elopment with his first wife - he had to steal her.)	
73.12.	"	Sally Johnson (His father's favorite)	
73.13.	"	Walk Along John (a favorite of his great-grand father)	
T-917			
74.1.	Almeda Riddle	Mama Buy Me a Chiny Doll	Rte 3, Box 122 Heber Springs, Ark
A 74.2.	"	Go Tell Aunt Nancy	
A 74.3.	"	Chick-a-la-li-lo.	
74.4.	"	Nishi Had a Mama	
A 74.5.	"	My Little Rooster	
74.6.	"	Green Gravel	
74.7.	"	The Hangman's Tree	
74.8.	"	The Merry Golden Tree	
74.9.	"	Rainbow Mid the Willows	
T-918			
75.1.	Almeda Riddle	The House Carpenter (needs patching)	
75.2.	"	The Titanic	
75.3.	"	The Lonesome Dove	
75.4.	"	Poor Wayfaring Stranger	
75.6.	"	Alan Rein.Edit. In first perf.second stanza ommited so first 2 are appended to the finish	

TAPE	PERFORMER	TITLE	ADDRESS	TIME
76.1.	Almeda Riddle	Texas Rangers (mistakes but well-sung)		
76.2.	"	Down in Arkansas XXX (needs repair)		
Dairy Camp, Parchman.				
76.3.	John Dudley	Clarksdale Mill Blues XXX	Rte 4, Box 114 Dundee, Miss.	
76.4.	"	*** dift, miking		
76.5.	"	You Got a Mean Disposition (cut last stanza)		
76.6.	"	I Ain' Goin' Down the Dark Road by Myself		
76.7.	Ervin Webb	I'm Gwine Home XXXX	42 N. Collet St Prichard, Ala.	3.1!
76.8.	Washington	My Jack Don't Drink No Water	Rte 1, Box 94-B Flora, Miss.	
	Bridges Lee Cole tenor J.T.Sanburn baritone		4315 Mississippi Ave, Gulfport, Miss. 854 Cherry St, Grenada, Miss.	
76.9.	Bridges Lee Cole	Cap'n,Doncha Know Me (holler made out of wksongversesx)		
76.10.	John Dudley	Cool Water Blues (and interview)		2.3C
76.11.	John Dudley	Poor Boy Blues XXX		2.3C
T-9>0				
Dairy Camp,Parchman []				
77.1.	Ervin Webb -voc Harold Blackman -guit ...	You'se One Little Wretch XX ......Box 183, Philadelphia,Miss.		2.C
77.2.	John Dudley	I'm Gonna Move To Kansas City XXX (Guitar break dull)		2.1
77.3.	John Dudley	Cool Water Blues XXX		2.?

TAPE	RECORDED	ALBUM	ADDRESS
	October 10th,1959.		
77.4.	Vera Hall Ward	No Room at the Inn	1227 19th St Tuscaloosa,Ala.
77.5.	"	Take 2.	
77.6.	"	Mamma Gonna Buy You a Little Lap Dog XXXX 3 4! (cut when "he's asleep now."	
77.7.	"	Take 2. XXXXX 40	
77.8.	"	Wild Ox Moan (Lots of b.g. noise)	
77.9.	"	Take 2 XXXXX (noise under final stanza) 5 on next tape is better)	
78.1.	Vera Hall	No Room at the Inn (n.s.g as take 2,75.5.)	
78.2.	"	I Got a Home in That Rock	
78.3	"	I'm Ridin' In a Buggy XXX		2.0C
78.4.	"	Boll Weevil Holler-from Rich Amerson (noise under 2nd stanza) XXX		2.4!
78.5.	"	Boll Weevil -take 2 (noisy) XXXX		2.0C
76.6.	"	Wild Ox Moan (must be repaired) XXXXX	
78.7.	Wade Derling	That's All Right	1227 19th St, Tuscaloosa, Ala.
78.8.	"	Old Speckled Lady Xx	
78.9.	Vera Hall	Trouble So Hard XXX		2.1C
76.10.	"	Young Speckled lady	
78.11.	"	Great Day		2.1C
78.12	"	Death, Spare Me Over Till Another Year (see ? tape)	

-cont-

A 79.1

TAPE	PERFORMER	TITLE	TIME
79.1.	Vera Hall	O Death Have Mercy xxxx	
79.2.	"	Take 2.	

Georgia Sea Island (St. Simon's Island)

TAPE	PERFORMER	TITLE	TIME
79.3.	Bessie Jones	Death Spare Me Over Another Year xxxx Rte 4, Box 22.SSI	
79.4.	Whole group	O Mary Doncha Weep X good sound	1.30
79.5.	Bessie lead with gp	You Better Mind How You Talk xxxx good sound	2.30
79.6.	Peter Davies 1d	Rock in the Weary Land xxxx good sound	2.00
79.7.	Bessie solo	Go to Sleepy Little Baby -1 xxx -2 xxx........	.45 / 1.00
A 79.8.	"	The East Coast Line xxx	.35
79.9.	"	Sometime & explanation xxx	.50
A 79.10.	Willis Proctor 1d	Pay Me My Money Down	2.05
79.11.	"	You Got My Letter	2.00
79.12.	Joe Armstrong 1d & John Davis	Riley xxx	
A 79.13.	John Davis 1d	John the Band xxxxx	1.30
79.14.	John Davis 1d	O Raggy Levee	2.10
79.15.	"	O Raggy Levee -2 xxxx	1.05
79.16.	"	Carrie Belle	2.10

The Group: Bessie Jones, John Davis, Arnold Road, House 504;
Willis Proctor, Demere Road; Joe Armstrong; Henry Morrison; Peter Davies;
Jerome Davis; Ben Ramsey.

T-983

TAPE	PERFORMER	TITLE	TIME
80.1.	John Davis 1d	Carrie Belle -11 xxxx	2.15
80.2.	Henry Morrison 1d then John takes	Hop Along, Let's Get Her xxx 2 takes	.45 / 1.00
80.3.	Willis Proctor 1d	Adam and Eva in the Garden X (good sound) with shouters & patters	1.40
80.4.	John Davis 1d	Moses Don't Get Lost	2.10
--cont--			

TAPE:	PERFORMER:	TITLE:	ADDRESS:	TIME
				.2
				.2
				.2
79.2.				2.0
80.5.	Willis Proctor 1d	Adam in the Garden xxxxx		2.1
80.6.	John Davis 1d	Moses Don't Get Lost xxxxx		2.00
80.7.	Willis Proctor 1d	Read 'Em, Johnny xxxxx		1.45
A 80.8.	John Davis & Bessie Jones	Blow Gabriel xxxx (Judgement Bar) with thing + clapping		2.00
80.9.	Willis Proctor 1d shout	Talk Believer, Daniel xxxxx		2.00
80.10.	" short	Adam in the Garden xxxxx		1.45
80.11.	Willis (?) short	Kneebone xxxx		2.00
80.12.	" short	Goodbye, Everybody xxxx		2.00
80.13.	John Davis 1d short	Blow Gabriel (Judgement Bar) Judgement		4.00

T-981

TAPE	PERFORMER	TITLE	TIME
81.1.	John & Bessie	Judgement Bar (attach to previous box)	4.00
81.2.	Willis & Bessie	Eli, You Can't Stand xxx	2.15
81.3.	Willis 1d	One of These Days xxx	2.25
81.4.	Bessie 1d	Daniel in the Lion's Den xx	2.30
81.5.	Henry Morrison 1d	Lazarus X	1.30
A 81.6.	Henry Morrison 1d	I'm Gonna Sail Like a Ship on the Ocean xxxx	2.30

T-982

TAPE	PERFORMER	TITLE	TIME
A 82.1.	Bessie vocal, Charles Gaskin -dance	Hambone	1.10
82.2.	group (+Bessie)	Buzzard Lope	1.45
82.3.	group and ??	Prayer, leading into Sign of the Judgement X	2.10
82.4.	woman & gp	Everyone's Talkin' 'Bout Heaven X	3.30
82.5.	Ruth Odell & gp	He Never Said a Mumblin' Word X	2.30
82.6.		On Calvary	2.45
82.7.		Down By the Riverside	2.98
82.8.	Bessie gp	Little David -two takes xxx first long false	2.98
--cont--			

TAPE:	PERFORMER:	TITLE: a little more formal	ADDRESS:
82.9.	John Davis & SD	Live Humble — Good - March'50	.45
82.10.	Henry Cohen & SD	Wade in the Water	2.00
82.11.	Willis Proctor	Run to the Rock — Good (not shaking)(Sinner, You Can't Hide)	
82.12.	John Davis	My Lord's Gettin' Ready ForThat Great Day (tape ran out)	2.0

Group 2 members: George Cohen, Rte 2, Box 115; Ruth Ozell, Rte 2, Box 11
Leola Harris, Rte 2, Box 119; Jerry Harris, Rte 2, Box 119;
Viola McQueen, Rte 2, Box 116; Emma Lee, Rte 2, Box 114.

These six people paid three dollars each as an advance.

1-9-76			
83.1.	John Davis & SD	On That Great Day(cont. from previous box)	
83.2.	Jerry Harris	Daniel In the Lion's Den(poor)	
A 83.3.	Bessie 1d	Johnny Cuckoo X X X	2.0
83.4.	Bessie 1d	Throw Me Anywhere, Lord(Buzzard love) X X X	1.5
83.5.	"	Take 2	

1-9-7	J.J. Mainer Band		
A 84.1.		Johnson's Old Grey Mule voc.E.J.; 3 guit;fiddle; bass;banjo.	
84.2.	"	Take 2 (two guits only this time)	
84.3.	Carolyn & EJ voc	Three Nights Drunk(fiddle;2 guit;banjo;bass.)	
84.4.	Carolyn & Mary voc& guit	Columbus Stockade2 guit;fiddle;banjo;bass.	
84.5.	"	Take 2.	
A 84.6.	band	Whoa Mule (banjo lead;3 guit;bass)	
A 84.7.		Glen's Chimes (banjo lead;3 guit; bass;fiddle)	
A 84.8.	E.J. Vocal	Train Hundred and Eleven (and band)	

Band: J.J. (Joseph Emmett) Mainer, fiddle and vocal,264,Poplar Tent Rd,
Concord, N.C.; Larv Mainer, guitar & vocal, same address;
Jim Dillon, guitar, 301 West 22nd St, Kannapolis, N.C.; Floyd Overcash,
bass, Rte 2, Stanfield, N.C..; Carolyn (Mainer) Holmes, guitar & vocal,
44 Mainer's Drive, Concord; and Glenn Mainer, banjo, 264 Poplar Tent Rd.

Index

Photo: Katie Vandyck

About the Author

Shirley Collins is a stalwart of the English folk scene with a singing voice of unparalleled tender beauty. Although no longer performing, she regularly lectures and appears on radio as an authority on traditional music. Recently *Within Sound,* a 4-CD box set of Shirley's recordings, was released on Fledg'ling records to great critical acclaim.

In 2004 she was awarded the Gold Medal by the English Folk Dance and Song Society for services to English folk song.

www.shirleycollins.co.uk

About the field recordings

In the early 1930s, Alan Lomax and his father, pioneering folklorist John A. Lomax, first developed the Library of Congress' Archive of American Folksong as a major national resource. The Alan Lomax Archives represent an exceptional assemblage of audio and videotape, 16-mm film, photos, published recordings, and assorted papers documenting folk music, dance and ritual from around the world.

The Archives were created over the course of 60 years symbolising the lifelong determination of Lomax to recognize the artistic achievements of worldwide local cultures.

www.culturalequity.org

www.safpublishing.com

info@safpublishing.com